The Films

of the

Dionne Quintuplets

D1447306

The Films

of the

Dionne Quintuplets

Paul Talbot

BearManorMedia.com

Published by:

Bear Manor Media
PO Box 71426
Albany GA 31707

www.bearmanormedia.com
Book Design by Leila Joiner

Printed in the United States of America on acid-free paper

ISBN 978-1-59393-097-4
ISBN 1-59393-097-6

For my mother and my Godmother

✦ Table of Contents

FIVE STARS ARE BORN 9

THE COUNTRY DOCTOR 15

REUNION 43

THE QUINTUPLETS HONE THEIR TALENTS 57

FIVE OF A KIND 63

THE QUINTUPLETS RETIRE FROM SHOW BUSINESS 81

FILMOGRAPHY 85

BIBLIOGRAPHY 97

INDEX 101

In the 1930s Twentieth Century-Fox mogul Darryl F. Zanuck produced a trio of hit features starring the most popular team of the decade. The movies' stars were so beloved that Bette Davis, after seeing them in person, told the press that she would refuse to appear in a film with them because they would steal all the scenes. Although their three pictures are almost completely forgotten today, the Dionne Quintuplets were the highest-paid film performers of the era and the most pampered stars in movie history.

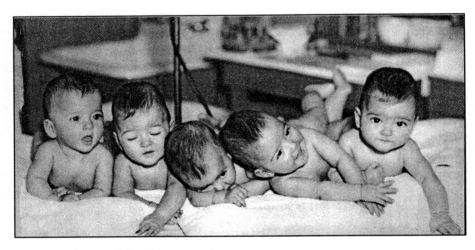

THE DIONNE QUINTUPLETS, LATE 1934
LEFT TO RIGHT: EMELIE, CECILE, MARIE, ANNETTE, YVONNE

✦ Five Stars Are Born

The five movie stars were born on May 28, 1934 in a small farmhouse in the rural town of Callander in Ontario, Canada. In the very early morning, young Elzire Dionne went into labor and summoned midwives Alexandre Legros and Benoit Labelle. As Elzire's husband, Oliva, left to fetch Dr. Allan Roy Dafoe, the midwives delivered two tiny, misshapen babies. Dafoe arrived as a third infant was being born and, assisted by the two midwives, delivered the final two. On that night it seemed impossible that the five baby girls would turn out to be adorable box-office attractions. In Pierre Berton's book, *The Dionne Years*, the first born quintuplet is described as "the tiniest infant the two midwives had ever seen: a grotesque creature with the legs of an insect and a disproportionately large head, bright blue in color and scarcely human except, oddly, for the large eyes with the long lashes and an appreciable shock of hair." Dafoe would later say that the newborns looked like "five little French frogs" and "like rats."

The total weight of the sickly, premature baby girls was a mere ten pounds, and Dafoe did not expect any of them, or their mother, to survive. But after being warmed in the oven, fed drops of rum, rubbed with olive oil, and packed closely in a basket, the tiny sisters slowly became healthy. The five identical babies were true miracles; only three other sets of quintuplets had been recorded, and all of those infants had died within hours.

Oliva Dionne, who already had five children to feed, was stunned by the quintuplet birth and had no idea how he would support them. At the advice of his priest, Dionne accepted an offer from an American promoter who wanted to exhibit the infants, alive or dead, at the Century of Progress Exhibition in Chicago. The press got wind of the deal and presented Dionne as a cruel monster willing to exploit his precious miracle babies. Public outrage against the father grew so strong that Canadian political leaders made the five children wards of the government and created a guardianship to handle the babies' health and business affairs.

Among the appointed guardians was Dafoe, the doctor who had nurtured the Quintuplets to health. The widowed, fifty-one-year-old country doctor had been in Callander for more than twenty years and had delivered 1,400 babies. Dafoe was private, reclusive, and completely unknown, but he would soon become the most famous doctor in the world and the subject of three major motion pictures.

At three months old, the Dionne Quintuplets (Yvonne, Annette, Emilie, Cecile, and Marie) were taken from the family farmhouse and moved across the dirt road to become the only "patients" at the brand-new Dafoe Hospital. The facility was mobbed constantly by ever increasing crowds demanding to get a glimpse of the famous babies. To appease the masses, a schedule of twice-daily free public exhibitions of "the Quints" was established. The unknown town of Callander soon became a major tourist destination as millions from all over the world came to see the girls and to spend money at ho-

THE QUINTS GURGLE INTO A MICROPHONE FOR A
DECEMBER 1934 RADIO BROADCAST.

tels, gas stations, gift shops, and food stands. The area became known as "Quintland."

Dozens of companies, desperately wanting to capitalize on the Dionne Quintuplets, assaulted the girls' guardians with numerous endorsement offers. The Quints' handlers were offered a flat $50,000 fee for all advertising, still-picture, and movie rights, but they wisely decided to negotiate each deal separately.

Exclusive world rights to the girls' still photos were bought by the American syndicate Newspaper Enterprises of America (NEA) for $10,000 a year. Fred Davis, the Quints' official photographer, shot the girls, often alongside Dafoe, daily for one hour each morning, ultimately producing thousands of stills, including all those used in advertising. Six hundred and seventy-two daily newspapers in the United States subscribed to the photos and the five girls' ubiquitous cheerful images were welcomed by millions of Depression-era readers. In their 1963 autobiography, *We Were Five*, the sisters wrote: "Posing for photographs was as much a part of our lives as the careful brushing of teeth…There was no end to the demand for Quintuplet pictures…The result was that we celebrated every holiday from New Year's Day to New Year's Eve weeks in advance, so that the photographs could be sent out in good time to NEA customers."

Within days after the astonishing birth, cameramen from Pathe and Fox-Movietone, the two leading newsreel units, had descended upon Callander to fight for exclusive motion picture rights. Pathe ultimately won the deal and appointed Canadian Roy Tash as the girls' official newsreel photographer. The Pathe deal, which was based on a percentage, paid the Quints up to $15,000 per short.

On October 19, 1934, once the babies' health was stable, their first short subject, a one-reeler called *A Day in the Lives of the Dionne Quintuplets,* was shot. Cameraman Tash described the filming in an article for *The International Photographer*: "Their eyes must be protected and a minimum amount of light must be applied. If I should make the lights the least bit 'hot,' for back-light effects, etc., this may spell trouble. Their daily routine must not be interfered with in making these pictures. Remember, their health is the first consideration…"

In addition to being shown in theaters, where it was often billed above the main feature, *A Day in the Lives of the Dionne Quintuplets* accompanied Dafoe's December 1934 lecture at Carnegie Hall and the Dionne parents' February 1935 Chicago vaudeville tour. ("Here are the pictures the world has

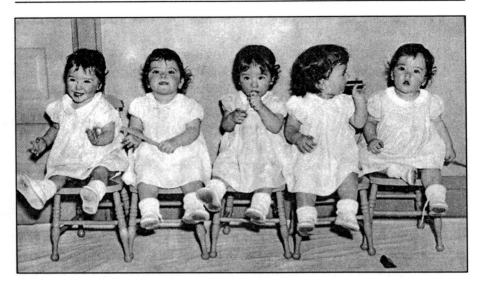

THE DIONNE QUINTUPLETS AT TWENTY-MONTHS-OLD, JANUARY 1936. LEFT TO RIGHT: MARIE, ANNETTE, EMELIE, YVONNE, CECILE.

been waiting to see!" roared the announcer.) About the parents' stage tour, the magazine *Movie Mirror* wrote: "It didn't last long, because after so many uneventful years in the quiet backwoods the Dionnes couldn't be expected to be sparkling or fascinating as actors. When one had looked at them for a minute or two, he had seen all there was to see."

Soon the Dionne Quintuplets were a marketing phenomenon. The girls and Dafoe received hefty licensing fees to appear in ads for dozens of products, including Lysol, Colgate Dental Cream, Quaker Oats, Carnation Milk, Palmolive Soap, Puretest Cod Liver Oil, General Motors, Karo Syrup, McCormick's Biscuits, Baby Ruth candy bars, and Musterole Chest Rub. The girls' likeness appeared on paper dolls, coloring books, radios, hair ribbons, safety pins, sheet music, typewriters, playing cards, calendars, suckers, and dresses. Dafoe's fame increased when he signed up for his own radio show and a ghostwritten newspaper column in which he gave homey medical advice. The doctor also made guest appearances on the Eddie Cantor and Rudy Vallee radio shows.

Members of the Hollywood elite were not immune to the Quints' charms. James Stewart and Bette Davis each made a trek to Quintland, while little Shirley Temple, then ranked as the number-one movie star in the nation, told a *Photoplay* interviewer that she wanted Santa Claus to bring her the Quintuplets for Christmas. Radio stars talked about the Quints, while onscreen Groucho Marx and the Three Stooges made cracks about them. During the 1934 Christmas season, the famous babies made their radio debut in a special recording for the Canadian Broadcasting Company that featured Dafoe speaking over the baby talk.

In May 1935, Canadian radio listeners could hear the Quints celebrating their first birthday party as Dafoe narrated recordings of the toddlers taking a bath and being tucked into bed. The guardians hoped that a regular radio show starring the Quints would be possible when the girls got older. Pathe produced and released a second short subject, *The Dionne Quintuplets at Play*, the same year, and it was only a matter of time before Hollywood decided to incorporate the Dionne Quintuplets into a major studio feature.

Fellow book lovers Jean Hersholt and Dr. Allan Roy
Dafoe in the doctor's library during the production of
The Country Doctor.

✦ The Country Doctor

Charlie Blake, a reporter for the *New York Journal* and *Chicago American* newspapers, was one of the first to cover the Dionne story. Two days after the birth, Blake arrived in Callander with a kerosene incubator that Dafoe desperately needed to keep the babies alive. Earning the doctor's gratitude and trust, Blake wrote many articles on Dafoe and the Quints. "As we talked," Blake later wrote in an article for *Photoplay*, "the thought first came to me that here was a new 'country doctor' story with a great climax…in fact a quintupleted [sic] climax. I outlined the story, a purely fictional life of a fictional country doctor, and shipped it to Hollywood where it was shipped back quick. Sometimes with thanks and sometimes in the same envelope in which it left Chicago. Last summer [1935] Harry Brand, the press agent deluxe for 20th Century-Fox, wanted Dr. Dafoe to come to Hollywood to act as a technical director for one of their pictures. A handsome piece of change was offered plus the lure of a trip around North America by boat. I passed the offer on to 'doc' and he, as usual, said: 'No thanks.' I reported Dr. Dafoe's refusal to Harry Brand in a letter and concluded it with my shopworn outline of the 'country doctor' story." The young writer's three-hundred-word outline ended up in the hands of Darryl F. Zanuck.

Zanuck had been appointed head of production for Twentieth Century-Fox in 1935 after the merging of Twentieth Century Pictures and Fox Films. Always searching newspapers and magazines for suitable movie material, Zanuck was well aware of the Dionne Quintuplets and paid Blake $5,000 for the outline. Zanuck believed that the film would be a perfect vehicle for Fox contract star Will Rogers, a top box-office draw, who had previously expressed interest in playing a country doctor in a movie. "I obtained a temporary release from my paper and went to Hollywood for the great adventure," Blake recalled.

Although the tireless Zanuck had complete control over all Fox productions, he realized that he could not possibly be involved with every single aspect of every picture and created a system where each picture would have an "associate producer" who would personally manage each project according to Zanuck's strict guidelines. To supervise *The Country Doctor,* the mogul chose writer-producer Nunnally Johnson, a former journalist who worked briefly for Paramount before being hired by Zanuck to write such Fox hits as *Moulin Rouge* (1934), *House of Rothschild* (1934), and *Prisoner of Shark Island* (1936). Johnson later recalled, "I suppose I took [the job] because Zanuck asked me to and if he'd asked me to jump off the bridge I'd have done it. I had a great regard for him…and, of course, being a producer sounded as if I had more control. I didn't really have a great deal more control, because Darryl at that time was in charge of everything."

To transform Blake's brief outline into a screenplay, Zanuck assigned Sonya Levien, who already had forty-five pictures to her credit and, at $1,600 a week, was one of Hollywood's best-paid writers. Levien's previous screen-

plays for the rural-set *Rebecca of Sunnybrook Farm* (1932) and *State Fair* (1933) made her an appropriate choice for a project about a small-town doctor. In fact, back in November 1930, Levien had written an unrelated outline for Fox called "The Country Doctor," and while that project never reached the screenplay stage, she reused some story elements in the Dafoe project. Johnson, Blake, and Levien met with Zanuck in one of the mogul's legendary marathon script conferences, after which, armed with Zanuck's extensive notes and a fistful of news clippings on Dafoe and the Quintuplets, the trio began the screenplay.

DOROTHY PETERSON, JEAN HERSHOLT AND DR. DAFOE STROLL IN THE CANADIAN SNOW DURING A BREAK FROM SHOOTING *THE COUNTRY DOCTOR.*

The production suddenly lost its lead actor on August 15, 1935

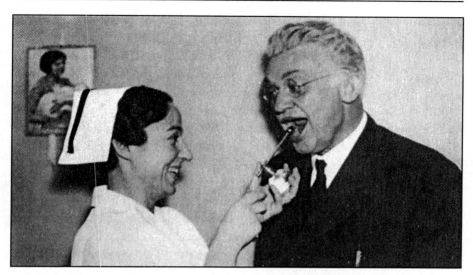

NURSE YVONNE LEROUX DISINFECTS JEAN HERSHOLT'S THROAT ON
THE SET OF *THE COUNTRY DOCTOR*.

when Will Rogers was killed in a plane crash in Alaska. "I felt the world had suddenly dropped away," Levien later wrote. "I was so moved by [Rogers'] death, that the idea came to me to tell the story from the point of view of a simple country doctor trying to cope with this amazing thing."

While the first draft was being written, Zanuck searched for a director from among the studio's roster and decided on Henry King. In the business since 1912, King had been a director, producer, writer, or actor on more than eighty pictures, including *State Fair* and the silent hits *Tol'able David* (1921) and *Stella Dallas* (1925). Shortly after joining Fox, Zanuck had heard from several associates that King had a reputation for taking too long on his pictures, and had considered dropping the director's contract. When King heard the rumor, he went to Zanuck himself and offered to leave the studio. But Zanuck felt that King's small-town upbringing and the subject matter of some of his earlier pictures made him appropriate for *The Country Doctor*. King agreed to complete the picture on schedule so that the studio could capitalize on the Quintuplet phenomenon, and he got the assignment.

"For five weeks," Blake wrote, "Sonya Levien had patience with me as we worked out the first 'rough draft' of the 'country doctor' story." Blake provided most of the details relating to the title character. Like the real-life Dafoe, the doctor in the screenplay was a lover of dogs and detective stories, refused money from patients, and had an affluent physician brother. Written as modest and saintly, the doctor was shown at one point turning down a $10,000 product endorsement. (In reality, Dafoe accepted many lucrative licensing deals.) For her part, Levien added subplots dealing with the doctor's loyal nurse, a bumbling constable, and two young lovers. The writers called their doctor "John Luke" and set the story in the fictional rural Canadian community "Moosetown." In a memo to Levien, associate producer Johnson said that her script was "a superb job. To me you have captured completely the picture of Dafoe that we wanted to present. I can scarcely imagine it being done better." But Zanuck demanded that the love scenes be expanded and that the dialogue be modernized.

King also had ideas on how to improve the story and got together with Johnson and Levien for an intense ten-day conference. The director and Levien met for one more day until 2:00 a.m. with a stenographer recording their discussions. Johnson, a comedy specialist, added humor to the script while King, an aviation buff, was probably responsible for deciding that the

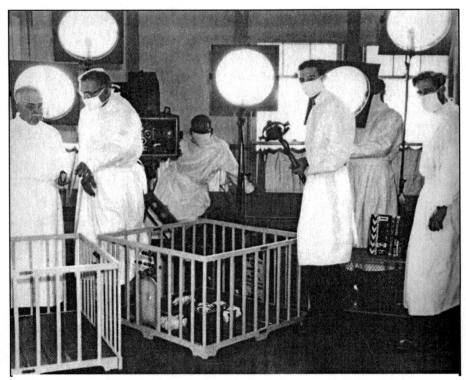

DR. DAFOE (FAR LEFT) SUPERVISES THE STERILIZED CREW DURING
THE FILMING OF THE DIONNE QUINTUPLETS'S SCENES IN
THE COUNTRY DOCTOR.

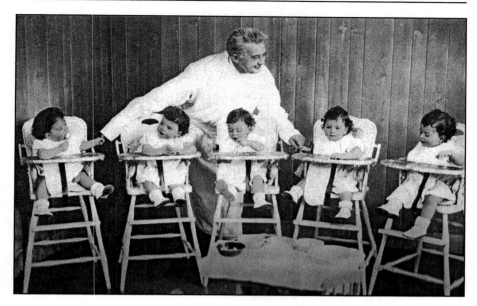

JEAN HERSHOLT WAS REQUIRED TO WEAR A HOSPITAL GOWN WHILE
POSING FOR THIS PUBLICITY STILL WITH THE FIVE
TOP-BILLED STARS OF *THE COUNTRY DOCTOR.*

male romantic lead would be a pilot. Johnson then gathered all of the written material and wrote the final draft himself, reportedly within a week. Levien would end up receiving the sole screenplay credit, while Blake was credited with "story idea suggested by."

Realizing that *The Country Doctor* now needed another star to replace the hugely popular Rogers, Zanuck decided to add not one, but five big names. He wanted the Dionne Quintuplets to play themselves.

But Zanuck wasn't the only one that wanted to sign the Quints for a feature. Screen legend Mary Pickford, who had first-hand knowledge about the public's fascination with child movie stars, met with the guardians about producing a movie with the Quintuplets. One of the guardians, Judge J. A. Valin, told *Movie Mirror,* "[Pickford] is a Canadian respected by us all. She would make a fair and square bargain, and I believe the Quintuplets would benefit financially to a great degree by any arrangement made with Miss Pickford."

Also hoping to sign the Dionne Quintuplets for their feature debut was Paramount Pictures, who wanted the toddlers to appear with Harold Lloyd in

The Milky Way. For the brief cameo, as babies who receive a delivery from milkman Lloyd, Paramount offered $25,000.

Fox read about Paramount's plans for *The Milky Way* in the September 28, 1935 issue of *Motion Picture Herald.* Blake recalled: "We heard the report at four o'clock in the afternoon and at midnight I was flying toward Toronto for a conference with Ontario's Minister of Welfare David A. Croll [one of the guardians], Dr. Dafoe and Joseph Sedgwick, the deputy attorney general of Canada. [Also present was New York Twentieth Century-Fox executive Joseph Moskowitz and the girls' business manager, Keith Munro.] …The meeting…started at noon on a Saturday and concluded at two the following afternoon."

As Sedgwick later recalled in an interview for the book *The Dionne Years,* "All the movie people were after us. We didn't know anything about that kind of deal what we should go for. [Pickford] said, 'Whoever you deal with get it in cash! Get the most you can, but don't take any overages or royalties because you won't get it back.' We made the deal [with Fox] because we kept in mind Mary's advice to get what you can in cash." The guardians insisted on a flat sum for the babies to appear in the feature and refused Fox's offer of a box-office percentage. The intense meeting finally concluded with the Dionne Quintuplets set to receive a whopping, record-setting acting fee of $50,000 to appear briefly in *The Country Doctor.*

It was the most lucrative deal yet for the five famous babies. The sum was enough to pay for the expenses of their private hospital for three years. As usual, Dafoe also got a cut. Fox paid him $10,000 for the rights to his life story and also awarded him a hefty fee to "supervise" the filming of the babies.

Although the guardians and Fox had agreed upon a price, the deal stalled when Pathe, whose newsreels were distributed by Fox rival RKO Radio Pictures, claimed that any Dionne Quintuplet features would infringe on Pathe's exclusive rights, which included all motion pictures. Pathe was finally pacified when Fox offered to license outtakes from the Quint newsreels to use in the feature. Final contracts for the Dionnes' appearance in *The Country Doctor* were signed in November 1935, with shooting to commence the following month. As part of the terms, all footage of the Quints would have to be shot inside the Dafoe Hospital.

With Rogers dead and no other Fox star suitable for the lead, King suggested Jean Hersholt. The Danish-born character actor had been in pictures since 1906, including *The Four Horsemen of the Apocalypse* (1921), *Greed*

(1925), *Grand Hotel* (1932), *The Mask of Fu Manchu* (1932), and *Dinner at Eight* (1933), and had previously worked with King on *Stella Dallas*. Hersholt's thick dialect had slowed his career when talkies arrived and Zanuck was leery of the actor's heavy accent, but reluctantly accepted King's choice. At forty-nine, Hersholt was only three years younger than Dafoe, and with dyed gray hair, a bushy moustache, and identical spectacles, he was easily made up to resemble the real thing.

Dorothy Peterson was chosen to play Katherine Kennedy, the doctor's hardened, but loving, nurse. The actress had been playing minor roles since 1930, most notably in *I'm No Angel* (1933), *Treasure Island* (1934), and *Peck's Bad Boy* (1934). Hersholt and Peterson were the only actors required by the script to actually appear onscreen with the Quints.

Wanting to put the picture into release as soon as possible to recoup the huge investment paid to the Quints, Zanuck sent King, Hersholt, Peterson, and a crew to Callander in early December to shoot the baby scenes. The nineteen others included Johnson, Moskowitz, cinematographer Daniel B. Clark, three cameramen, assistant director Robert Webb, three sound engineers, a script girl, a chief electrician, and a generator man. Also along were Levien and Blake, who continued to revise the script while on the train.

DIRECTOR HENRY KING CONSULTS WITH REAL-LIFE NURSE YVONNE LEROUX WHILE SHOOTING AN EXTERIOR SCENE FOR *THE COUNTRY DOCTOR*.

During the three-thousand-mile train trip from Hollywood to Canada, numerous reporters and news photographers met with the moviemakers to discuss the first feature that would star the Dionne Quintuplets. Before a single frame had been shot, the picture had become highly publicized and anticipated.

Arriving in Canada, after crossing the borderline at Port Huron in Michigan, the crew, accustomed to sunny California, was surprised by a snowstorm and the ten-degrees-below-zero temperature. After stepping off the train, the company was halted by a group of Canadian authorities, who informed them that local union technicians had filed a protest objecting that the film was being made with a Hollywood crew. The company was allowed to proceed with the six scheduled days of filming only after Moskowitz agreed to hire half a dozen Canadian technicians to supplement the Hollywood skeleton crew.

CECILE PUSHES A CARRIAGE WITH QUINTUPLET DOLLS IN THE
SHORT, *THE QUINTUPLETS' SECOND CHRISTMAS*.

GEORGE CHANDLER PROVIDES COMIC RELIEF WHILE MICHAEL
WHALEN AND JUNE KENT SUPPLY THE LOVE INTEREST FOR
THE COUNTRY DOCTOR.

Prior to the first day of shooting, King, Hersholt, and Peterson met with
Dafoe and two of the Quints' nurses, Yvonne Leroux and Cecile Lamoureux,
to discuss the handling of the now-seventeen-month-old babies. "When I
was first chosen for *Country Doctor*," Hersholt told *Picture Play* magazine, "I
was scared, for I thought, 'Suppose [the babies] don't like me, suppose they
don't take to me, how will I ever be able to play the part?'"

Before working on *The Country Doctor*, Dafoe knew absolutely nothing
about moviemaking and had seen only two movies in his life: the 1931 British musical, *Sunshine Susie*, and the first Quint newsreel. Hersholt recalled
his first meeting with Dafoe for *Woman's Home Companion*:

"I don't know you from Adam, Mr. Hersholt," Dr. Dafoe said with that
diffident smile that charms everyone. "But, please, that means nothing. I
know no one in pictures."

"Surely you've heard of Greta Garbo!" I protested.

"Who's she?" said the doctor.

Meanwhile, Clark received tips from Fred Davis, the girls' exclusive still
photographer. The interior stills and newsreels of the Quints had been pho-

tographed with hot movie lights that were heavily diffused with screens and blue glass in order to protect the babies' eyes. Clark, who had been shooting pictures since 1922, including Westerns and Charlie Chan movies, had recently spent weeks in Hollywood testing a special blue filter on babies who were the same age as the Quints.

"Without wholly copying Dr. Dafoe, I tried to transfer his personality intact to the screen," Hersholt told *Movie Classic* magazine. "I duplicated his mannerisms with pipe and hands. His manner of speech. I must have been successful at creating the illusion, for even my personal friends thought that the man in the first scene of that picture was not I but Dr. Dafoe."

At 9:00 a.m. on December 4, 1935, the first day of shooting, the crew parked the vehicles half a mile from the facility and quietly carried the equipment to the basement, where they waited until the stars awoke. The babies rose at their regular time (unlike all other movie stars, who often had to arrive on set before dawn) and completed their morning feeding and dressing rituals before crawling in front of the cameras.

Dafoe was constantly on set to enforce the strict guidelines that he had specified in the contract. All of the camera and recording equipment had to be sterilized, and the crew, after washing with a special soap, had to wear soft-soled shoes, gloves, hospital gowns, and face masks while they were in the hospital. In an interview for the 1978 documentary *The Dionne Quintu-*

SLIM SUMMERVILLE, JEAN HERSHOLT, AND DOROTHY PETERSON IN *THE COUNTRY DOCTOR.*

JOHN QUALEN'S ALREADY-SUBSTANTIAL BROOD IS ABOUT TO GET
FIVE ADDITIONS IN *THE COUNTRY DOCTOR*.

plets, Henry King recalled: "We looked like we were performing an operation instead of making a picture." King was restricted from holding the Quints or manipulating their reactions or expressions.

Hersholt and Peterson had to have their costumes sterilized and their nostrils and throats sprayed with a bitter antiseptic before they could interact with their tiny fellow performers. The crew could only spend thirty minutes setting up and thirty minutes breaking down the equipment each day, and the actual filming could only take place between 11:00 and 12:00 each morning during the six days. The technicians were burdened further by having to set up their equipment in the hospital's small rooms.

The first day's shoot lasted forty-nine minutes and dealt with Peterson singing "Jack and Jill" and combing Marie's hair while Yvonne jumped in her crib. Peterson, the first "outsider" to ever hold a Quint, was nervous while handling the babies but was able to complete her scenes. "I am not a sentimental woman," Levien said at the time. "Yet when I watched these five little girls dressed, one by one, I wanted to handle them, to snuggle them. I wanted to put them all in a giant basket and take them home."

Hersholt recalled: "The first glimpse I had of them was of the five of them sitting in five baby chairs against a wall. I was dumbfounded to see five copies of the same baby…When I realized that I was working with the five most famous babies in the world and that the doctor whom I was supposed to impersonate was watching me I was so nervous I blew up in my lines and spoiled the whole scene. All the scenes taken that first day had to be re-shot; the retake was made days later, and by that time I had become more accustomed to the idea of working with the quints."

For the next five days, the baby stars created some predictable problems. Their noisy giggling or crying would often drown out the dialogue of Hersholt and Peterson and on one day the sisters were so uncooperative that only four minutes of footage got filmed. Blake recalled: "On two days, Cecile became very temperamental…she refused to play with her sisters and for a short time on each of these two days, it looked as though the Quintuplets might be quads. But in the end Cecile perked up her little nose and joined in the jubilee. Not once but a score of times, director King would place the children in position where they would appear with their pseudo nurse and doctor, but before the camera could start to grind, all five of the girls would be in five different parts of the room…Dan Clark had to erect a fence around the tripod holding his cameras to prevent the babies from bee lining [sic] it to the tripod in an effort to climb the legs." Each day's priceless, unprocessed footage of the Quints was insured for $25,000 and shipped back home to the Fox laboratory where it was stored in a steel vault.

Hersholt told *Movie Mirror*: "Out of that entire company no one so much as sneezed while we were in Canada; everyone's first thought was for the health of the babies…and if the Quints didn't wake up then we just gathered our equipment and went back to the hotel, rather than disturb their program."

Although Dafoe dismissed the five stars each day at noon, shooting didn't completely stop. King was often able to grab some quick close-ups of Hersholt and Peterson, and later the crew was sent outside to collect some shots of the snowy countryside. Interviews with the press and the taking of Quintless publicity stills filled up more idle time.

The crew lost one day of shooting with Hersholt when the actor, wandering outside while waiting for the babies to awaken, slipped in the snow and got a severe bruise on his left leg. Dafoe ordered his impersonator to stay in bed for a day, and the incident provided the Fox publicity people with a nice still of the "real" doctor tending to the "reel" doctor.

Oliva and Elzire Dionne, angered at losing control of their babies, were bitterly estranged from Dafoe and did not visit the hospital during the week of filming. The parents had been in newsreels about their daughters, but they refused to appear briefly as themselves in *The Country Doctor* and even turned down Fox's offer of $700 merely for the use of their names. So instead of playing themselves, the Dionne Quintuplets played "the Wyatt Quintuplets" in the film, although each girl's real first name was used. Universal Pictures had signed the Dionne parents to play themselves in a movie called *Where Are My Children?*, but the picture was canceled when Elzire became pregnant with her eleventh child. Zanuck told the Dionnes that he would offer a movie contract if the birth produced more quintuplets.

With six days of Quint filming in the can, the *Country Doctor* crew headed back to Hollywood to complete the feature. For less than six hours of "acting" the babies had collectively made $50,000. Hersholt came home with a valuable collector's item: a doll-shaped wooden whistle that had been teethed on by his little co-stars. He told the press, "This little whistle is my most valuable possession."

The press reported that Yvonne and Emilie had grown new teeth during the shoot and that because the shape of their mouths had changed drastically, not all of the footage would match. But the initially nervous Zanuck saw no problems with the footage of the babies. The raw dailies of the Quints, as well

DOROTHY PETERSON HANGS FIVE DIAPERS IN A PUBLICITY STILL FOR
THE COUNTRY DOCTOR.

DOROTHY PETERSON AND THE QUINTS IN THE CLOSING SHOT OF
THE COUNTRY DOCTOR.

as the completed script, were sent to the guardians for their approval, which
was granted.

Zanuck, anxious to cash in on the public's anticipation for the movie, informed King that *The Country Doctor* had to be delivered to theaters in
March 1936. Not only would the remainder of the feature have to be brought
in for $650,000, but six days would be cut from the planned thirty-four-day
shooting schedule. Undaunted, the workaholic director plunged ahead.
Meanwhile, the impatient public could enjoy the Pathe documentary short,
The Quintuplets' Second Christmas, which was then playing in theaters.

Newcomers June Lang and Michael Whalen, as the love interests, were
joined by former Keystone Kop Slim Summerville as the bumbling constable;
veteran heavy Robert Barrat (*Captain Blood* [1935], *The Last of the Mohicans*
[1936]) as the mean-tempered manager of the town's logging company;
Montagu Love (*Don Juan* [1926], *The Cat Creeps* [1930]) as the pompous Sir
Basil Crawford; Frank Reicher (*Mata Hari* [1932], *The Invisible Ray* [1936])

as Dr. Luke's more prosperous physician brother; George Chandler (*Footlight Parade* [1933], *The Kennel Murder Case* [1933]) as a comedic pilot; and Jane Darwell (*The Scarlet Empress* [1934], *Curly Top* [1935]) as a matronly nurse.

Unable to secure an appearance by Oliva Dionne or even the use of his name, the moviemakers created the equally androgynous sounding "Asa," beefed up the father character as a comedic supporting role, and cast contract player John Qualen in the part. In pictures for only five years, Qualen had appeared in more than two dozen features, including *Our Daily Bread* (1934) and *The Farmer Takes a Wife* (1935). The actor was a similar age and physical type as the real-life Papa Dionne; with an added Charlie Chaplin-like moustache, the resemblance was very close. Playing on the public's interest in Oliva Dionne's fertility, the screenwriters used the father as a constant source of comic relief. ("I guess Old Faithful's spouted again!" cracks a nurse as Asa delivers the news that his wife is expecting once again.)

Frequent bit player Aileen Carlyle (*This Side of Heaven* [1934]), who was plump like the real Elzire Dionne, was cast in the virtually nonexistent role of the Quints' mother. The character has no first name and no lines; she only

THE BABIES RECEIVED HUGE OVER-THE-TITLE BILLING IN THE ADS FOR *THE COUNTRY DOCTOR*, EVEN THOUGH THEY ONLY APPEARED BRIEFLY IN THE LAST TEN MINUTES.

appears in one shot and a newspaper photo based on the famous first news photo of the real Quints and their mother. Like the real Dionnes, the movie parents already have a brood of children.

With his technical crew providing solid production values, Henry King finished shooting the picture on budget and even several days ahead of schedule. Cinematographer John F. Seitz, one of the highest paid in the business, filled in for Clark on several scenes. As the picture was being shot, the Quints' footage and the Hollywood-shot footage were gathered and cleverly cut by editor Barbara McLean, one of the few female editors of the era. (McLean later became the head of Fox's editing division and won an Oscar and seven other nominations.)

Finishing the movie with breakneck speed (footage was still being shot in late January), Fox held a preview on February 26, 1936 with a print that ran 110 minutes. After the preview, McLean cut the picture down to 94 minutes while the publicity department finalized the marketing campaign.

In the final version, the Quintuplets don't show up until one hour and eighteen minutes into the movie, but before they do, *The Country Doctor* has plenty of entertainment for its Depression-era audience: sappy romance, aviation scenes, drama and pathos, and a barroom fistfight. The climactic birth scene, in which the babies are born two months premature (like the real Quints), is an extremely well-written scene with excellent performances by both Summerville and Qualen, as each becomes more and more flabbergasted at the nonstop birth. ("You sure there ain't any more?" asks the stunned father, to which the nurse sighs, "Aren't you ever satisfied?")

When the top-billed stars finally appear, their screen time adds up to a whopping total of ten minutes, which includes the shots lifted from Pathe newsreels. The footage, which attempts to give equal time to each baby, starts with newsreel outtakes of the girls being bathed and fed, having their teeth brushed, and crawling around on the floor. The Fox-shot footage consists of the babies pounding their spoons on their highchairs, crawling in a crib, and rolling on the floor with Hersholt. Much of this documentary-like footage, which often goes out of focus, is silent, with Hersholt's and Peterson's voices dubbed over it. Many of the shots go on for a long time, and one stays on screen for a full minute. Apparently Zanuck wanted to make sure that the audience got their money's worth after having to wait so long for the stars to appear. Like true movie stars, the Quints get the final shot all to themselves when, after Hersholt looks directly into the camera and declares "miracles do happen," the quintet is shown gazing out a window and into the audience.

PUBLICITY STILL WITH JEAN HERSHOLT AND DOROTHY PETERSON
LOOKING INTO A CRIB THAT SUPPOSEDLY HOLDS THE STARS OF
THE COUNTRY DOCTOR.

Although the babies are in less than ten-percent of the movie, the credit "The Dionne Quintuplets in" appeared above, and in larger letters than, the title in the screen credits and in the advertising for *The Country Doctor.* A five-page announcement in the *Motion Picture Herald* told exhibitors that "Every newspaper in the country is a broadside for this show. For two years each gurgle of the quints has been red-hot news!" Other ads featured bally-hoo like: "The Greatest Youngsters in the World Bring You the Greatest Box Office Attraction You Ever Saw!," "It's the Most Blessed Event Since 'The Birth of a Nation'!" and "Quintuply Your Profits!" Large cardboard cutouts of each Quint were displayed in theater lobbies, and small photos of the babies in a wicker basket were handed out free to patrons. Lobby cards for the film depicted the girls frolicking in a basket and peering through a doorway, although they do neither in the film.

The Fox publicity staff, realizing that Dafoe was almost as big a name as the Quints, prominently placed the credit "Photographed under the personal supervision of Dr. Allan Roy Dafoe" on all advertising. In most ads, the doctor's name appeared in type size equal to that of star Jean Hersholt's. By this time, Dafoe was well known to moviegoers, having appeared in the Quint newsreels, including *The Quintuplets' Second Christmas*, in which he dressed as Santa Claus.

Among the promotional tie-ins for the picture was a photo-filled novelization and a tin of *Country Doctor* pipe tobacco that featured a shot of Hersholt, in character, smoking a pipe. King helped out with the marketing of the movie and traveled throughout the country to meet with exhibitors.

The most important *Country Doctor* tie-ins were the official Dionne Quintuplet dolls that were manufactured by the Madame Alexander Company. These lovely dolls had been released the prior Christmas and became huge sellers. Fox's pressbook informed exhibitors that the dolls could be purchased directly from the studio, and many theaters had a "free doll" contest. A Dafoe lookalike doll was also available, but it was simply called "Doctor" because Dafoe had not signed a contract for his name or image to be used.

Although movie publicity stills were always provided to newspapers free of charge, *The Country Doctor* was an exception. During the Canada shoot, the Fox still photographer was not allowed to shoot any stills of the Quints. All photos of the girls from *The Country Doctor* were taken by Fred Davis and were available for publication only if the newspapers paid the standard NEA fee of $50 each. Many publications balked at the fee and accompanied their reviews with alternate stills such as Hersholt holding five milk bottles or Peterson hanging five diapers. Like many of the other photos released by NEA, several of the publicity stills for the Fox picture had been created by pasting together two or more images since it was rare when all five babies would cooperate for the camera at the same time.

Fox opened the Quints' highly anticipated debut feature in the United States and Canada on March 4, 1936 in 326 theaters, including the elegant Radio City Music Hall in New York. A critic for *Time* called the movie "warm-hearted, amusing and astonishingly skillful cinema."

Variety predicted that the film was "A cinch to cop world-wide coin...a showmanship natural...the accumulated impetus of two years of intensive headline exploitation is behind the picture. How can it miss?...Dionne Quintuplets do not appear until the last quarter hour of the film. There's about 75 minutes of build-up. Which is a long time coming to the star of any show... Story moves and holds even while admittedly and recognizably merely scaffolding for the appearance of the Dionnes...*Country Doctor* is not without

ADVERTISING HERALD.

angles that might be considered weaknesses. First of all, there is not much footage…of the Dionnes; and their late appearance, a necessity for production purposes, may not be a word-of-mouth recommendation…The wide distribution of the newsreel stuff devoted to the quintuplets has possibly taken off some of the brightness of the picture's novelty. Even so, it is impossible to imagine *The Country Doctor* as anything but a box-office bull's-eye."

Frank S. Nugent of *The New York Times* began his review by stating, "We were prepared to disapprove of the quintuplets as a matter of policy, but there is no holding out against *The Country Doctor*." Nugent called the film "an irresistibly appealing blend of sentiment and comedy [which] justifies even that anonymous advertising genius who described the advent of the Dionne babies as the greatest event since *The Birth of a Nation*…there may have been funnier moments in screen history than those in which John Qualen becomes the astonished father of five, but somehow we cannot recall them… [T]his scene must go down in cinema history as one of its most priceless contributions to the gayety of nations…Qualen is quite the funniest father the screen has found…The authentic Dionne babies have a special place reserved for them near the close of the film…We suppose they are all right as an extra added attraction, but the truth is that the film would have been just as good with the quintuplets represented only by inference…Anyway, it's a mighty pleasant picture."

Influential publisher Paul Block, whose review appeared on the first page of each of his newspapers, wrote: "…we advise you to try to see this beautiful, wholesome picture of truth and romance, of laughter and tears…There is a great story told in this grand screen play…we thought *The Country Doctor* with the little quintuplets would be a picture just for mother and sister but we were wrong. Every man, woman and child will be better for having seen this screen production…" Fox reprinted Block's full review in a full-page ad in *Motion Picture Herald*.

More rave reviews came from the *Miami Herald* ("It is a privilege to sit through so magnificent a picture"); *Morning Eagle* in Lawrence, Massachusetts ("The most worthwhile picture in the history of the screen"); *Toledo News-Bee* ("One of those very rare vehicles that is worth seeing twice"); *New York Daily News* ("One of those inspired pictures which happens rarely in a life time"); *New York Daily Mirror* ("Looms as an immediate candidate for a leading place among the best ten pictures of 1936"); Bridgeport *Telegram* ("'Great' is the only adjective to describe everything about it"); *Portland* (Maine) *Express* ("This is one picture you simply must see"); *Los Angeles*

COVER OF NOVELIZATION.

Herald ("A grand, magnificent picture without the quintuplets; with them, it is sensational"); *New Haven Register* ("Much has been heard about the greatness of this picture. It does not disappoint"); *Hartford Times* ("The screen's proudest creation"); *St. Louis Post-Dispatch* ("One of the finest pictures that has come out of Hollywood"); *Milwaukee Sentinel* ("a picture every mother and daughter, every father and son will relish, because to see it is to love it"); and the *Pittsburgh Sun-Telegraph* (A masterpiece").

Audiences didn't seem to mind that only a small amount of footage was devoted to the Quints. According to *The Hollywood Reporter,* Fox enjoyed "one of the largest, if not the largest, day-and-date engagements in motion picture history."

In a letter to Dafoe, Levien wrote: "The most satisfying thing I have to report is the great success of our *Country Doctor.* I hope with all my heart that you have seen it and *like it.* In fact, I am so anxious on that point that I would appreciate hearing from you. I saw it with several audiences. They loved it. In all my twelve years of scenario writing—and I have written some of the finest pictures in the industry—I have never heard such enthusiasm on the part of the audiences." The doctor wrote back and called the movie "good fiction and full of human interests."

The stars' parents were not among the many that enjoyed the picture. Oliva and Elzire were invited by the studio to stay at the Waldorf-Astoria and see the film's premiere at Radio City Music Hall in New York. Elzire, who had previously seen only three movies in her life, was excited about seeing her babies on a big screen, but was angered by the movie's saintly depiction of the highly paid Dafoe. Oliva became enraged as the audience roared with laughter at Qualen's portrayal of him as a backwoods simpleton.

The Country Doctor also offended members of the Roman Catholic Church who were disturbed by the frank and comic portrayal of childbirth, and several Canadian political leaders, who disapproved of the stereotypical portrayal of the country's citizens and government leaders. None of this controversy had any effect on the picture's box-office success.

An unusual advertisement-editorial, signed by Twentieth Century-Fox president Sidney Kent, took up two full pages in the March 21, 1936 issue of *Motion Picture Herald* and read:

> There have always been in show business a few who envy anybody else's success. They take joy in spreading false propaganda about their competitors or their competitors' product.

It is unfortunate that a grand production, such as *The Country Doctor*, which is both a credit and an asset to the entire motion picture industry, should be the victim of this propaganda.

Certain people have gone out of their way to spread the rumor that this picture is flopping. We have a good idea who are behind it and it should be to their eternal shame.

For the benefit of those who bought the picture and who have still to run it, I want to quote a few statistics about one of the most successful pictures this business has seen in many a day:

The Country Doctor opened in 322 theatres between March 3rd and March 8th.

Of those theatres playing the picture for a week's engagement, 53 held *The Country Doctor* over for a second week or transferred it to another first-run theatre for a second week.

48 theatres extended their engagements from three to four days.

31 theatres extended their engagements two days, and 83 theatres found it necessary to play the picture an extra day.

In all, 215 theatres or more than 67 percent of the 322 that played the picture in its first week of release, held the picture over for additional playing time.

One of the most successful pictures released by Twentieth Century-Fox Film Corporation this year was Shirley Temple in *The Littlest Rebel*. Released on Christmas Day, it played during the holidays to enormous business.

The Country Doctor already has surpassed *The Littlest Rebel* in receipts by more than 15%.

Of course, there are individual spots affected by terrific weather conditions that have not done as well as the exhibitor might have hoped. We speak of the average.

We are proud to point to the chorus of critics' praise which has greeted the picture from coast to coast and from Canada to the Gulf. Not only have the motion picture reviewers accorded *The Country Doctor* their highest rating and most enthusiastic praise, but great publishers and editorial writers have gone out of their way to urge the American people to see this great human document.

We are not responsible for certain greedy individuals who hoped this picture would pay off the national debt. We are, however, humanly happy that *The Country Doctor* has brought profits to our customers, entertainment to millions and has been a credit not only to ourselves but to the entire motion picture industry.

This picture is a sincere contribution to the business we are all making our living out of. It is an asset to the cause of better pictures, no matter who turns them out.

This, then, is the record of *The Country Doctor*. These figures do not lie, and if this be a flop, we pray give us more like it.

The Dionne Quintuplets' debut feature continued to make money when it was released throughout the world later in the year. Ultimately grossing $1.4 million in the United States, *The Country Doctor* was Fox's second biggest hit of the year after *Lloyd's of London,* which was also directed by Henry King. (The studio's next four biggest hits were all Shirley Temple vehicles.)

The Country Doctor made Jean Hersholt into a star and earned him an improved Fox contract and a heftier salary. "I owe my new stardom to those babies," he told *Movie Classic* magazine at the time. "I have just rounded out my thirtieth year on the screen. Twenty-four of those years I spent in Hollywood, continually making pictures. That's a rather formidable record. But never in all my experience has one role had the reverberating effect on my career and on my personal life as has the playing of *The Country Doctor*. I find myself constantly addressed as 'Doctor' Hersholt. People don't seem to separate me from the man I am on the screen with the Quints. When Ruth Bryan Owen, the ambassador to Denmark, was recently in Hollywood, her new husband insisted on addressing me as 'Doctor.' When I disclaimed the title, he pointed out that to him I would always be that, since seeing me with the Dionne babies."

The Country Doctor also increased the fame of the Quintuplets and Dafoe. *Literary Digest* reported that the Quints were "acknowledged by the industry to be the greatest audience-drawing combine in the history of motion pictures." The magazine *Movie Mirror* predicted that "They'll continue to be screen luminaries so long as they remain the world's eleventh wonder…Five, ten, and fifteen years from now the Quints will still be smiling and laughing at us from the screen." The delighted Zanuck gave raises to both Nunnally Johnson and Henry King, who each went on to enjoy three decades and several Oscar nominations at the studio.

Zanuck planned a series of Dionne Quintuplets features that would be released annually to show the girls growing up. The mogul knew the potential of star personalities (earlier in his career he had made the dog Rin-Tin-Tin

THIS APRIL 1936 MAGAZINE COVER FEATURED AN
EARL CHRISTY PAINTING.

into a major box-office draw) and decided to add the Quintuplets to Fox's roster of "personality stars," which included Shirley Temple, Jane Withers, Alice Faye, and ice-skater Sonja Henie. Wanting a Quint follow-up immediately, Zanuck contacted the girls' guardians to set up a multi-picture contract.

The guardians were well aware of *The Country Doctor*'s success and knew that the babies' highly publicized appearance, despite its brevity, was what brought people into the theater. After negotiations, Fox agreed to pay $250,000 total for brief appearances by the Dionne Quintuplets in three more features. The Quints would also receive ten-percent of the movies' profits, plus a $50,000 bonus upon completion of the third picture. It was a sweet contract for the five sisters, who already had a quarter of a million dollars in the bank from their various business deals, and who were now the world's highest paid movie stars.

While Fox planned another feature for them, the Quints returned to movie screens in the Pathe short, *Going on Two*, which contained footage of them feasting on five birthday cakes. Newsreel cameraman Roy Tash recalled: "In making my pictures of the babies, the nurses…do most of the arranging of the children. Claude Collins, of Pathe, who is on the spot directing the action, has lost many a hair out of his head because at times the children do just what they shouldn't do when the camera starts running. Since they are *Going on Two*, incidentally the title of Pathe's last two-reel production on the 'Quints,' we find them harder to handle; I should say they are as active as a bunch of crickets. They won't stay 'Put' long enough to get shots of all five together. Needless to say that this runs into a lot of waste footage."

"Until a few months ago," Tash continued. "It was not so great a trick to pose the babies. We could set them on a table and wave a colored handkerchief or a shiny object at them to attract their attention and then steal the shot. To see us at work must be amusing, since we must act like circus performers to arouse their facial expressions. It is a common sight when we are making our shots in the nursery to see either Collins or myself trying to stand on our heads, balancing on one hand or peeping through the tripod legs making funny faces at the babies in order to cause emotion. These fool antics must be done quietly since the 'mike' is always open in order to catch all natural sounds…Our toughest shot was to get a picture of them all asleep and here we ran into some grief. Just as soon as I would click the camera motor on, one of the children would sit up to see what was going on…We finally succeeded in getting the shot after waiting a couple of hours when they were in slumber land."

By this time, the Quints had collected $90,000 from their deal with Pathe. The girls were also kept in front of movie fans' eyes by appearing on the covers of the April and July issues of the popular *Modern Screen* magazine. Cartoon versions of the Quints, designed by famous caricaturist T. Hee, appeared briefly in Fritz Freleng's 1936 Warner Brothers cartoon, *The Coo-Coo Nut Grove*.

THE DIONNE QUINTUPLETS WITH TWO OF THEIR REAL-LIFE NURSES AND DIRECTOR NORMAN TAUROG ON THE SET OF *REUNION*. THIS SCENE WAS NOT INCLUDED IN THE FINAL FILM, BUT PHOTOS OF THE GIRLS IN THESE OUTFITS WERE USED EXTENSIVELY IN THE ADVERTISING.

✦ Reunion

With the Dionne Quintuplets signed, Zanuck wanted a sequel to *The Country Doctor* in theaters for the upcoming 1936 Christmas season. After quickly soliciting story ideas, he chose an outline written by Bruce Gould, titled *They Always Come Back*. (During production, the title was changed to *Reunion*.) Gould's premise had Dr. Luke retiring after delivering his three-thousandth baby, while Moosetown threw a party attended by all of the people that he had brought into the world, including the Wyatt Quintuplets.

Zanuck again chose Sonya Levien to turn the raw material into a screenplay, but he was disappointed in her characters and dialogue and assigned a complete rewrite to Sam Hellman and Gladys Lehman, who had previously collaborated on the Shirley Temple vehicles *Little Miss Marker* (1934), *Poor Little Rich Girl* (1936), and *Captain January* (1936). Zanuck was not pleased with that duo's first draft either, and ordered a series of rewrites. Screenwriter Walter Ferris (*Lloyd's of London, Under Two Flags* [both 1936]) was also involved in the early stages of the writing but was not credited.

Nunnally Johnson was originally expected to return as the Quints' producer, but he was assigned to other projects. Instead of having just one associate producer to supervise *Reunion*, Zanuck chose Bogart Rogers, Harold Wilson, and Earl Carroll, three men who were new to movie production. Rogers had previously been associate producer on *Everybody's Old Man* and *Pigskin*

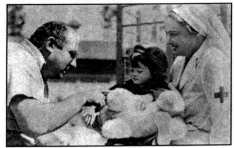

DIRECTOR NORMAN TAUROG, EMILIE DIONNE, AND DOROTHY PETERSON FILMING *REUNION*.

JEAN HERSHOLT, ROCHELLE HUDSON, AND TWO OF THE QUINTS
SHOOT A SCENE FOR *REUNION*. DUE TO CHILLY WEATHER, THIS
WADING POOL SCENE WAS NEVER COMPLETED AND HUDSON
ENDED UP HAVING NO SCENES WITH THE QUINTS.

Parade (both 1936), while Carroll and Wilson had the same duties on Temple's *Stowaway* (1936). Carroll, a personal friend of Zanuck's and a hit songwriter and hugely successful producer of Broadway showgirl revues, was working briefly at Fox during a career low point. For some reason, none of the three associate producers received an onscreen credit. Rogers was listed alone in the press credits while only Carroll and Wilson were billed on the posters and advertising graphics.

To direct the Quint sequel, Zanuck assigned Norman Taurog, who had been directing since 1920 and whose hits included *College Rhythm* (1934) with Jack Oakie and *Mrs. Wiggs of the Cabbage Patch* (1934) with W. C. Fields. Taurog won the Oscar for best director for *Skippy* (1931), mainly for the tearjerking performance that he had gotten out of his young nephew Jackie Cooper. Taurog was thirty-two at the time, and remains the youngest director to ever win an Oscar.

As with *The Country Doctor*, the first footage shot for the sequel was that of the Quints. It was originally announced that the Dionne Quintuplets would be photographed in color for their second feature, but *Reunion*, like their other features and shorts, was shot in black and white when it was determined that the strong lighting required for color would be potentially dangerous to the stars.

In an article he wrote for the magazine *Hollywood*, Taurog recalled: "Darryl Zanuck said to me on the day I was boarding a train in Hollywood bound for the little town of Callendar [sic], Ontario, Canada, and the Dionne Quintuplets, 'Norman, don't try to make them act. Just photograph what they can do. That's all I ask of you.'" The director and his crew of seventeen arrived in Callander in mid-August 1936 and began shooting the two-year-old Quints on the 17th, again for only one hour a day and according to Dafoe's strict rules.

Costume designer Luis Royer, who had previously designed wardrobe for Fox stars Temple, Alice Faye, and Sonja Henie, created special sunsuits, bonnets, and berets for the Quints to wear in their second feature. Months earlier, the studio had received specific measurements for each of the five stars, but by the time shooting started, the costumes were snug on the rapidly growing toddlers.

In addition to the returning Jean Hersholt (with darker hair) and Dorothy Peterson, who were shooting their second Quint feature in eight months, young Fox contract player Rochelle Hudson was also sent to Callander. Hudson, playing the same ingénue role that June Lang had created in *The Country Doctor*, had been in pictures since 1931, including *Imitation of Life* (1934), *Les Miserables* (1935), and four Will Rogers vehicles.

In the sequel screenplay, specific actions were written for each of the Quints to perform in three separate scenes, but the end result bore no relation to the suggestions made by the writers. A late screenplay draft introduced the Quints as follows in this excerpt:

MEDIUM FULL SHOT NURSERY
    The five little girls are in their nightgowns, kneeling beside their cots in an attitude of prayer.
    A French nurse is reciting the Lord's Prayer.

CLOSE SHOT ANNETTE
    Her hands are pressed together in prayer. She gently patty-cakes her hands. Camera moves to each of the others in turn. Emilie stares curiously at the nurse, Cecile crosses herself haphazardly,

Marie rests her head on her hand, Yvonne is studying her spread fingers. As the nurse finishes the prayer, the Quints cross themselves, leap to their feet, and clamor into their beds. Dr. Luke and [nurse] Kennedy cross to the first cot.

DR. LUKE
So you're coming through with that bicuspid, eh, Annette? Show me. Ouvre la bouche.

Annette opens her mouth wide. The other four girls have their mouths wide open, too.

DR. LUKE
It's through, all right!

The camera follows Dr. Luke's progress through the nursery. For each of the tots Dr. Luke has a word of greeting. Cecile is hiding from him under the bedclothes, to play hide and seek while Dr. Luke pretends to wonder where she has gone. Marie has put her feet on the pillow and the Doctor and his little ward have a gay time as he turns her about in her little bed. Emilie he admonishes for not staying in her bed at night. Annette gives him a toothy grin and Yvonne is fast asleep, her fists clenched above her head.

FADE OUT

The screenwriters wasted their time writing specific scenes like this. Once again Dafoe did not permit the director to manipulate the girls, and Taurog was only allowed to shoot what the toddlers did naturally. Even if Dafoe had been less strict, there was not much more that the director could have gotten out of the young movie stars. Like most offspring of multiple births, the Quints were slow to develop in their early years. Their speech was very limited, and their walking skills were also slightly impaired.

The baby footage for *The Country Doctor* had been shot in the dead of winter, forcing the movie crew to film exclusively inside. But because of the summer weather, much of *Reunion* was filmed outdoors at the Dafoe Hospital's recently built playground. Although still photographer Davis had determined that daylight was not harmful to the girls' eyes, cinematographer Daniel B. Clark once again used a special filter for the exterior scenes since harsh movie lights were still required.

Taurog had experience working with toddlers before, notably with one-year-old Baby LeRoy in *A Bedtime Story* (1933), but the Quints were hand-fuls. On some days, Taurog and the crew hid with the cameras behind bushes to try to catch the Quints acting naturally. Taurog recalled: "When the quints do appear, you've got to work fast and use every fleeting moment. And you mustn't upset them in any way. So, as they came into view, we turned the cameras loose and shot whatever happened...Limited to an hour a day, I must admit that we were terrifically handicapped in 'shooting' scenes with the Quints. Never having been disciplined, it was only natural that the little minxes did exactly as they pleased. If I particularly wanted the entire group in a scene, invariably one would have nothing to do with the idea, and by the time I might get the recalcitrant one persuaded, Doctor Dafoe would walk in, pull out his watch and say, 'That's all for today, boys.' My oral persuasive powers were limited, too, as I speedily discovered that the Quints didn't care

ROBERT KENT, ROCHELLE HUDSON, JEAN HERSHOLT, AND
DOROTHY PETERSON IN A PUBLICITY STILL FOR *REUNION*.

JEAN HERSHOLT AND SARA HADEN IN *REUNION*.

much for my alleged French, nor for my lullabies. Finally, I gave up directing them. One day I discovered that, like Baby LeRoy, they liked to pull off my glasses and throw them on the floor. Or, my watch did just as well. And they liked to tweak Jean Hersholt's mustache."

"Only once did I out-smart them," Taurog continued. "It was necessary to get a scene of them all going to bed together. The Quints have a very amusing habit of all racing for their beds simultaneously and plunging into them hit or miss. But, when they were supposed to quiet down and go to sleep, up they jumped, and away. I tore my hair frantically over this scene. It seemed impossible to get until I suddenly remembered that we were trying to film this scene in the late morning, after they had enjoyed a full night's sleep. They were wide awake, full of fire, and they didn't want to even pretend to go to sleep. So, I simply waited until the hour for their nap for my hour of 'shooting' and that was that."

The Quints' second appearance in the screenplay read: "People are watching the Quints in their pool, and are walking slowly along the passageway which is covered with felt and layers of cork to avoid the noise of footsteps. Four of the babies (in bathing suits) are playing in the pool. Standing by the pool are Dr. Luke, Kennedy, and Mary (in street clothes). The babies line up and look each other over. The four babies go to the dressing room. One of them opens the door and they look in. The fifth baby has a big powder puff and is dusting herself with powder. The five babies run back to the pool and continue to play. They have a rubber fish which is oiled so it will leap out of their hands when they try to hold it. One has a water toy which squirts water when pressed. Dr. Luke kneels beside the pool. One of the babies splashes water over him."

On the day the pool scene was to be shot, Taurog could not lure the girls into the pool until he sat, fully clothed, in the water himself. The director recalled: "Picture the scene of a rotund, erstwhile dignified director sitting in a wading pool while five delighted little girls gleefully poured water down his back! We couldn't 'shoot' with me in the scene. At the moment I had the Quints persuaded to play in the pool by themselves, while I made movies, Doctor Dafoe popped in to announce: 'Sorry, boys, time's up. No more pictures!' The next day the weather turned cold, and we never did get the scene." The scene's omission not only decreased the five stars' screen time, it also eliminated Rochelle Hudson's one scene with the girls and wasted the expense of sending the actress to Callander.

"I must admit that the scenes with the Quints tax my ingenuity as an actor as no other role I have ever played!" Hersholt told *Movie Classic*. "[I acted] with Emilie this morning, my pet by the way. I didn't know what she was going to do in the close-up but I had to anticipate everything she did and to improvise dialogue to fit! That dialogue, you must remember, had to match the rest of the story! And a mistake on my part would have lost us this scene. For there are no 'retakes' when you work with the Quintuplets. No chance of capturing the same mood with the self-same Quint twice…I work less than an hour each [day] with the babies, but I am completely exhausted at the end of it. Every minute is a terrific strain."

In a "making of" article for *Movie Classic*, Sonia Lee wrote: "In hospital gowns and masks, every man in the crew works as precisely as a bit of machinery. Not one lost movement with a concentration almost painful…Their foreheads are beaded with perspiration. Their lips white with effort…Cecile has been [Dorothy Peterson's] shadow since shooting began on this present location trip. For minutes on end she sits with this baby in her lap, slowly repeating one French word after another while Cecile struggles to imitate her."

Magazine advertisement.

"I'd like to spend at least six months with the Quints not making pictures but watching them, taking care of them, seeing them thrive," Peterson said. "I can't think of a more fascinating occupation."

While the pressbook claimed that the Quints were filmed for one hour a day, six days a week for *twenty-six days,* this must be ballyhoo since the brief footage that appears in the movie could not possibly have taken that long to shoot. The Quints' fee for playing in front of the cameras in their second feature was $83,000.

After the Callander shoot, Taurog returned to the Fox lot in Hollywood to complete the rest of the picture. While the crew shot in Canada, screenplay revisions had continued back at the studio with uncredited writer Jack Mintz creating some comedy sequences.

Although "thousands" of guests supposedly appear at Dr. Luke's retirement party, the screenplay only focused on a handful. The characters included a childless governor who ultimately adopts a young orphan; a faded actress hoping that a tie-up with the Quints will be good publicity; and a colleague of Luke's who fears that his much younger wife may be ready to leave him.

Returning from *The Country Doctor* were Slim Summerville, John Qualen, Montagu Love, and, in a different role, this time as a comic pickpocket, George Chandler. *Reunion*'s large cast also included Alan Dinehart (*Dante's Inferno* [1935], *Charlie Chan at the Racetrack* [1936]), George Ernest (*Destry Rides Again* [1932], *Little Men* [1934]), Helen Vinson (*I Am a Fugitive From a Chain Gang* [1932], *The Kennel Murder Case* [1933]), Esther Ralston (*Oliver Twist* [1922], *Peter Pan* [1924]), and Hattie McDaniel (*Judge Priest* [1934], *Show Boat* [1936]).

Former boxer Robert Kent took over as Dr. Luke's nephew. (Michael Whalen did not reprise the role.) A former contract player at Paramount, where he was billed under his real name of Douglas Blackley in pictures like *College Scandal* and *Car 99* (both 1935), the actor was signed to Fox after Zanuck discovered him in a stage play. Kent followed his Quint picture with Fox's *Dimples* (1936) with Shirley Temple. In the article, "Hollywood's White Hopes," *Movie Classic* described the actor as: "A tall, quiet-spoken lad…Everybody over at Twentieth Century likes him. He's a sincere worker. He's modest and has no illusions of grandeur about himself. You'd like him, if you knew him," and chose Kent as one of "a dozen or more young actresses and actors who will in this coming season of 1936-1937 reach stardom in pictures." Kent, who ended up with bit roles or parts in "B" pictures, didn't succeed like James Stewart, Tyrone Power and Don Ameche, who were also on the list.

When Qualen heard that Oliva Dionne had been offended by his portrayal in *The Country Doctor,* the actor sent a letter to the Quints' father explaining that he was just following the script and meant no offense. He also enclosed a dollar and asked for an autographed photo of the famous father. Dionne sent Qualen the photo, but the Papa character was once again presented as a buffoon, and Dionne was once again offended.

Shooting continued on the Fox lot through late October, with much of the filming taking place outdoors and dozens of extras appearing in the party scene. As an additional birth-related gimmick, Hersholt was shown greeting nine sets of twins and a set of triplets at the banquet.

Jack Murray (*The Prisoner of Shark Island,* 1936) edited the movie and reshuffled several scenes from the order in which they appeared in the screenplay. Although *Reunion* was still being shot in late October, Fox completed the post-production quickly and previewed the film at a suburban theater in Hollywood on November 20, 1936.

A reviewer for *Motion Picture Herald* who saw the preview wrote: "Naturally the film's biggest exploitation factor rests in the Dionne Quintuplets... Important as are the youngsters from an entertainment and commercial standpoint, they are not, however, the entire show. Even were they eliminated, the actual story told in the film would be a subject of audience and exhibitor interest...It is sound entertainment in every phase."

In *Reunion,* the Dionne Quintuplets first appear fourteen minutes into the 81-minute film and are seen for two minutes climbing into their cribs, throwing their toys, and tugging on Hersholt's stethoscope. Fifty minutes later, Hersholt wraps up his retirement party speech by announcing, "And now the real guests of honor are arriving." The Quints then pull up in five pony-driven carriages, slide down a slide, play with toy instruments, and have a tea party with milk. Real-life Dafoe Hospital nurses, including Yvonne Leroux, Jacqueline Noel and Mollie O'Shaughnessey, played themselves in this sequence. The toddlers appear in *Reunion* for a total of approximately eight minutes, the least amount of screen time of their three features. It is the only Quint vehicle that doesn't feature the sisters in the closing shot.

The remainder of *Reunion*'s running time deals with a love triangle, adultery, a suicide attempt, boyhood fistfights, and adoption, while Summerville and Qualen again provide welcome comic relief. This time Asa is afraid that his fame will be diminished because the constable's wife will have sextuplets.

ADVERTISING HERALD FEATURING THE QUINTS
IN COSTUMES NOT SEEN IN FILM.

("It wouldn't be fair for Jim to have six, seeing as how we're neighbors and all.") Like the real-life papa Dionne, Asa appears to have profited from his fame and is seen in tailored suits. The mother character doesn't appear and isn't even mentioned.

Reunion is the weakest of the Quints' three features. Moviegoers who saw *Reunion* and weren't familiar with the Dionne Quintuplets and/or hadn't seen *The Country Doctor* must have had a lot of questions: Why are these children being kept in "Dr. Luke's Hospital for the Quintuplets?" Do they have a rare disease? Is their father a widower?

Reunion opened at the Roxy in New York on November 27, 1936, and was released throughout North America for the holiday season. Many theaters didn't accept passes for the prestigious feature. As a gimmick, female theater employees were costumed as Red Cross nurses.

Fox's massive promotional push once again had "The Dionne Quintuplets in" splashed over the title on posters, lobby cards, and marquees. One advertisement boldly oversold *Reunion* as "the most unusual and suspenseful picture ever made...with the year's most important cast...highlighted by the most uproarious comedy the screen has ever seen!" The December issues of *Photoplay, Screen Romances,* and *Movie Classic* all had articles on and photos from the movie, including many stills from the aborted wading-pool sequence. A photo from that nonexistent scene was also used on one of the lobby cards.

Another vignette with the Quints was apparently unfinished or edited out of the feature. Exterior stills of the girls wearing rompers and berets, including a shot of Taurog directing Emilie, were used extensively in the *Reunion* advertising materials. But the girls wear no such outfit during their two scenes in the final movie.

Once again, official Dionne Quintuplets dolls were sold in theater lobbies. Available as accessories were recreations of the outfits that were designed for *Reunion.* Publicity photos showed co-stars Jean Hersholt and Rochelle Hudson holding the dolls. During the 1936 holiday season, the Quint dolls outsold the hugely popular Shirley Temple dolls and at the Dafoe Hospital, the Dionne Quintuplets were given dolls of themselves for Christmas.

Although the stars of *Reunion* were only two-and-a-half years old, children in Chicago were forbidden to see the movie. The picture dealt with the unmentionable subject of childbirth, so the city's board of censors restricted the audience to "Adults Only!" and the film was blacklisted by the local Legion of Decency.

Like most sequels, *Reunion* did not fare as well with the critics as *The Country Doctor* had. *The New York Times* reported that "[T]he Dionne quintuplets are running through their limited but endlessly fascinating dramatic repertoire at the Roxy this week…They bring with them, perhaps, too numerous a supporting cast of grown-ups, for the truth is that *Reunion* is pretty regrettable, as much for the superfluous adult presences on the screen as for the too frequent and too long absences of the Callander glamour girls. Of

WINDOW CARD.

course, it is almost impossible not to have story trouble when leading ladies are 2 years of age and five in number, but serializing the quints in annual chapters was Mr. Zanuck's idea, and he has only himself to blame if he is stuck with it…The parents, it is interesting to note, have been almost wholly discontinued. The mother does not appear at all; the father is a comical, forgotten man…The humorous incidents involving Constable Slim Summerville are less humorous than might have been expected. Only the Quints themselves can be endorsed without reservations."

An equally unimpressed reviewer for *Variety* wrote "This follow-up on the first story of the Dionne quintuplets is too episodic to command interest or suspense, but it probably will appeal in no lesser measure to the same class of patronage that flocked before to see the famous babies…Some women may think it all very cute, but it will not appeal to the men…The two episodes of the children are intrusive, but apparently welcome…Comedy is not stressed, but sufficient." In Canada, the *North Bay Nugget* complained that the "footage allotted the babies left much to be desired."

Although not a blockbuster like *The Country Doctor*, *Reunion* was still a hit and justified the Quints' huge fee. Zanuck announced that Shirley Temple would co-star with the Dionne Quintuplets in a future picture, but the team-up never happened.

"Aside from the new success the babies have made possible for me, they color every day of my life," Hersholt said at the time. "I receive letters from mothers who ask advice about their children. Hundreds of letters have come to me…solely concerned with the Quints. 'What do they eat? What are they really like? Are they truly beautiful?'"

✴ Between Features:
The Quintuplets Hone Their Talents

Nineteen thirty-six was a hugely profitable year for the five Canadian toddlers. In addition to having two hit movies, popular dolls based on their likeness, and dozens of product endorsement deals, they were being seen live by five thousand visitors per day. Twenty million dollars was spent on visiting the Quints in 1936 alone. In early 1937, when it came time to renegotiate the girls' still-photo rights, the NEA photo service had to pay $50,000 to keep their exclusive deal.

In May 1937, during the heavy media promotion for the Quints' third birthday, Fox announced that production would begin soon on *Mother Knows Best,* the third feature starring the Dionne Quintuplets. But a month later Zanuck reconsidered his plans and halted the pre-production. The mogul was well aware that child star careers were short-lived and that "personality vehicles" had to be carefully developed to prevent repetition and audience boredom. With two movies left on the costly Quint contract, Zanuck couldn't depend on audiences to keep buying tickets if the stars did nothing more than tip over chairs or bang on toy pianos in every picture. Hoping that in another year the Quints would be able to sing and dance instead of just wander in a playground, Zanuck decided to hold off before putting the toddlers into another feature. (Quint references continued to appear in other studios' films, such as the 1937 Disney short, *Pluto's Quin-Puplets.*)

NEWSPAPER AD FOR 1937 SHORT.

AD FOR HOME MOVIE RELEASE OF THE 1937 SHORT,
A DAY AT HOME.

Despite having to wait before appearing in another feature with the Quints, Jean Hersholt immediately continued playing a country doctor, albeit with a different name. CBS signed him to play the title role in the radio serial *Dr. Christian*, which began in 1937 and ran for seventeen years. He also played the role in a half-dozen movie programmers for RKO that were made from 1939-1941.

Although they were seen on motion picture screens by millions of people and were viewed live by millions more, the three-year-old Dionne Quintuplets never left their private hospital and had very little interaction with other people. Other than themselves, the girls only had contact with Dafoe, their parents (who reportedly visited infrequently), their nurses, and Dr. William Blatz, the child psychologist who studied them. Like many children born prematurely and siblings of multiple births, the Quints were tardy in developing their vocal skills. They communicated among themselves using sounds and gestures like, according to Blatz, "a flock of birds would do." Blatz described the sisters' individual personalities as: "Yvonne – most motherly; Annette – most aggressive; Emile – most independent; Cecile – most unpredictable; Marie – most sympathetic." Although even the nurses had trouble telling the girls apart, everybody who came in contact with the Quints were won over by their pleasant personalities and charm.

When the Quints played outside during their twice-daily exhibitions, they were viewed by tourists through glass that had been diffused with wire in an attempt to prevent the girls from knowing that they were being watched. But the sisters could hear the murmurs of the crowds and see the human outlines through the glass. Decades later, the sisters recalled in an autobiography: "Those one-way screens were, in truth, two-way screens. We could always see through them, as one can see through frosted glass. We were always conscious of being watched, but we did not mind it in the least. Anyone wearing white showed up best...Almost without exception, we trusted everyone, family, friend or stranger, equally."

The Quints developed extroverted personalities and enjoyed performing in front of the crowds. Blatz noted: "The most striking thing that is apparent to anyone who has had the privilege of being in the Hospital and being with these five children is their friendly and happy attitudes towards each other and towards the staff."

Although they were taking a break from starring in features, the girls continued to appear on movie screens via their frequent Pathe-RKO documentary shorts. The cute short, *A Day at Home*, was shown in theaters in

1937 and was released to the 16mm and 8mm market later in the year by Pathegrams, Inc., the home movie division of Pathe. Projector owners were encouraged to "Show the Dionne Quints in Your Home This Christmas!" and "Bring the world famous five into your own home!" (The prices ranged from $1.00 for a 25-foot silent version to $30.00 for a 350-foot "Deluxe [sic] Sound Edition.") The charming short shows the five sisters waking up, brushing their teeth, pulling on Dafoe's mustache, napping on rugs, eating at their ta-

COVER OF 1938 PHOTO BOOK WHICH FEATURED THE QUINTS
ACTING OUT NURSERY RHYMES.

Humpty Dumpty

A RECREATION OF "HUMPTY DUMPTY" FROM THE 1938
PHOTO BOOK, DIONNE QUINTUPLETS PLAY MOTHER GOOSE.

ble, painting, drinking milk, playing with doll carriages, talking on the phone to Dafoe, saying their prayers, and falling asleep in their cribs. *A Day at Home* was undoubtedly a delight to theatergoers that loved children and a chore for those that did not.

Another Pathe short, *Quintupland*, which featured the girls frolicking in the snow and billed them as "The Dionne Darlings," was released to cinemas in early 1938. Film critic B. R. Crisler of *The New York Times* wrote: "The only movies we are able to sit back and enjoy in absolutely uncritical bliss are Chaplin comedies, Silly Symphonies and any picture at all about the quintuplets."

The Quints' still photo acting skills were put to use in *Dionne Quintuplets Play Mother Goose,* a picture book released by Dell Publishing in 1938 that featured the girls (separately and combined) in seventeen reenactments of classic nursery rhymes like "Humpty Dumpty," "Old King Cole," and "Rock-a-Bye, Baby."

In her memoir, *Quint to Queens,* nurse Louise Corriveau wrote: "There was never any resistance [from the girls] toward picture-taking, whether done for a serial film or in any other form. Not knowing that they were famous or the reasons for the pictures, it was just another game to them." Another nurse, Cecile Michaud, recalled: "They were little mimics, beautiful actors. They just loved to pose for pictures. There were no problems with that at all. They were full of joy and laughter all the time." One of the Quints' favorite games was for one of them to operate an imaginary movie camera while the other four acted in front of it. Because the girls obviously enjoyed posing for the still and newsreel cameras, it seemed possible to the guardians and Zanuck that the Dionne Quintuplets could evolve into genuine movie stars who could actually act and perform.

⋆ Five of a Kind

In early 1938 Zanuck decided to move forward with a third Dionne Quintuplets feature. To insure profitability, especially since the Quints were set to receive a $100,000 fee, Zanuck assigned the picture to Sol M. Wurtzel, the head of the studio's highly prolific "B" unit. A former bookkeeper, Wurtzel had produced several hit "A" pictures for Fox, including *Bright Eyes* (1935) with Shirley Temple, *Steamboat 'Round the Bend* (1935) with Will Rogers, and *Dante's Inferno*, before being appointed executive of the "B" unit

FLYER FOR OLIVA DIONNE'S SHOP IN CALLANDER. THE SHOP WAS RECREATED FOR A SCENE IN *FIVE OF A KIND*.

after Zanuck was named company head. The "B" unit cranked out a steady stream of profitable, secondary pictures including the popular Jane Withers, *Mr. Moto*, and *Jones Family* series. Reportedly an unpleasant and difficult ruler, Wurtzel delivered his pictures on short schedules that often ran only twelve to fourteen days and on tight budgets usually between $75,000 and $200,000.

Wurtzel assigned the writing of the new Quint project, then called *Everybody's Sweethearts,* to Lou Breslow and John Patrick, a duo that had already scripted fourteen screenplays for the Fox "B" unit, including *High Tension* (1936) with Brian Donlevy, *The Holy Terror* (1937) with Jane Withers, and *International Settlement* (1938) with Dolores Del Rio. Breslow had also directed a number of shorts, including *Punch Drunks* (1934) with the Three Stooges.

Working quickly, and using the then-popular "rival reporter" clichés, Breslow and Patrick came up with a scenario involving male and female American journalists who each try to sign the Wyatt Quintuplets to an exclusive radio contract. The pair fall in love, and the Quints sing and dance via live television for a benefit show in New York. (The Dr. Luke character was now a supporting role and had little to do with the story.) Although Breslow and Patrick were required to do several drafts, their screenplay was the only Quintuplets feature that didn't involve input from numerous successive writers.

Originally scheduled as director was the busy Alfred L. Werker, helmer of more than two dozen features including *House of Rothschild* (1934) with George Arliss and *Stolen Harmony* (1935) with George Raft. But Werker was replaced by the less experienced Herbert I. Leeds after Wurtzel saw *Keep Smiling*, a Jane Withers vehicle that Leeds had just directed. Impressed by the performance that Leeds had gotten from the young Withers, Wurtzel felt that the director would also work well with the little Dionnes. Leeds had directed two other "B" pictures for Fox: *Island in the Sky* with Gloria Stuart and the *Jones Family* entry, *Love on a Budget* (both 1938). Although publicity releases at the time reported his age as twenty-seven, the former editor was actually ten years older.

LEFT TO RIGHT: SCREENWRITER LOU BRESLOW, DR. ALLAN ROY DAFOE, JEAN HERSHOLT, FOX EXECUTIVE JOSEPH MOSKOWITZ, AND DIRECTOR HERBERT LEEDS DURING THE PRODUCTION OF *FIVE OF A KIND.*

Meanwhile, at the Dafoe Hospital, Yvonne, Annette, Emilie, Cecile, and Marie prepared for their most challenging movie roles yet. Hoping to have five new Shirley Temple clones in the Fox house, Zanuck instructed the guardians to teach the girls to sing and dance. (The Quints had already performed brief simple dances in some of their newsreels.) Nora Rouselle, who had recently been hired at the Dafoe Hospital as a nurse and teacher, began to teach the French-speaking Quints some simple English phrases and songs that could be performed in the picture.

The Quints' parents, who hated their daughters' movies anyway, were furious when they heard that the girls were being taught English for the film. At this point the animosity between the parents and the guardians was heated, and Oliva Dionne sought to regain custody of his famous daughters. By this point, the Quints' papa had also become a financially successful celebrity and owned the largest Dionne Quintuplets souvenir shop in Callander, where his personal autograph was available for a quarter.

To enhance the musical routine planned for the Quints to perform in the picture, Zanuck assigned studio songwriter Sidney Clare and musician Samuel Pokrass to create a tailor-made song. Best known for the standard "Ma, He's Making Eyes at Me," Clare had also written songs for Shirley Temple, including (with Richard Whiting) her huge hit, "On the Good Ship Lollipop" from *Bright Eyes* (1934). Clare tried to create a hit for the Quints and came up with "All Mixed Up," which included lyrics like:

> I'm "Yvonne."
> Ah! Go on.
> You forget
> That you're "Annette."
> Five little kiddies
> All mixed up.
> We'll find out from mother.
>
> Ooo ooo
> Who are you?
> I am "Emilie."
> I'm "Cecile."
> I'm "Marie."
> Oh! I'm not me.

Clare's lyrics and a recording of Pokrass' accompanying music were shipped to the Dafoe Hospital for the little girls to practice.

Studio costume designer Helen A. Myron, who had made dresses for Jane Withers, traveled to Callander well before the shoot to take the girls' measurements and found that there was only a one-fourth-inch height difference between Marie, the shortest Quint, and Yvonne, the tallest. Myron created five outfits for the girls to wear in their third vehicle, including suede "Swiss Miss"-type costumes with feathered caps, which was the garment featured

JEAN HERSHOLT WITH THE QUINTS IN *FIVE OF A KIND*.
THESE "SWISS MISS" OUTFITS WERE FEATURED PROMINENTLY
IN THE ADVERTISING.

most often in the publicity materials. To save time, the costume dresses were specially designed to close with one zipper instead of with multiple, cumbersome buttons. The five girls were dressed identically in every scene in the picture, just as they were every other day of their young lives.

Daniel Clark photographed a Dionne Quintuplets feature for a third time and penned an article about the experience for *American Cinematographer*. "Director Herbert Leeds and I went up to Callander a full two weeks before shooting commenced," the cameraman wrote, "not only to confer with Doctor Dafoe as to what should and should not be done, but to familiarize ourselves with the location and to familiarize our five little starlets with us! To my surprise and pleasure, the youngsters remembered me from my two previous visits."

In June 1938, a Fox crew arrived in Callander and began shooting the new feature, now called *Five of a Kind*. Wurtzel, who had several dozen other pictures in various stages of production, did not go to Canada. Fox executive

Joseph Moskowitz (who had finalized the *Country Doctor* deal) and location manager R. C. Moore handled the on-set production details.

Jean Hersholt went back to Canada to act with the sisters once again. (Although Dr. Luke's retirement was the premise behind *Reunion*, the doctor apparently changed his mind. In the third movie he is still in charge of the Quints and still making emergency house calls.) The actor had revisited the Dafoe Hospital ten days prior to filming in order to re-bond with the girls. In an interview for *Picture Play*, Hersholt said: "The last time I saw them, they were two years and three months old. They were cute, like little puppies, but their personalities had not yet developed. Now they are four years old, but the change in them in every way is so great that it is immeasurable…I had expected the quints to change, of course, in the twenty-one months that have elapsed since I last saw them, but I never thought that the change would be so astounding …And it is now harder to identify them than it has ever been. I used to be able to pick out Marie easily, for she was the smallest of the group. But now there is so slight a difference between her and the others I can't tell them apart. Perhaps if someone were to put them in a row and I could study them real hard, I could tell, but not when they are at play."

"One thing I am very happy about," Hersholt added, "is the friendly attitude Oliva Dionne, their father, showed toward me on my recent visit to

JEAN HERSHOLT AND HIS FIVE COSTARS HAVE A TEA PARTY IN *FIVE OF A KIND*.

THE QUINTS SAW PUPPIES FOR THE FIRST TIME AND JEAN
HERSHOLT FOR THE LAST TIME WHILE SHOOTING *FIVE OF A KIND*.

Callender [sic]. On previous visits, he remained aloof. But when I got to Callender [sic] recently, Mr. Dionne's business manager said that he wanted to see me. Wondering why he had sent for me, I went to the souvenir shop where he sells all kinds of toys and souvenirs and postcards connected with the quints. I discovered that the reason he sent for me was that he wanted to know if he could watch the filming of the quint sequences for *Five of a Kind*. He had never before watched the quints making a full-length movie. Of course we were only too glad to have him do so. We would have been glad to have his wife watch, too, but she is very shy. Hoping to please Mr. Dionne, I asked for a picture of the quints, although I have many pictures of them at home. He found one [and] autographed it to me…'How much is it?' I asked. He smiled.'For you nothing,' he said."

Dorothy Peterson did not return with Hersholt to shoot a third appearance with the Quints. (Although Dr. Luke didn't stay retired, his loyal nurse apparently did.) This time, the girls were attended to onscreen by a younger nurse played by pretty Marion Byron, best-known for Buster Keaton's *Steamboat Bill, Jr.* (1928). Byron, whose other credits were mostly limited to bits, was married to screenwriter Lou Breslow, who was also present for the Callander shoot.

The Fox unit, once again limited by not being able to shoot outside the confines of the hospital grounds, shot the Quints' sequences from June 6 through 21. "The task of filming the quints is a real technical problem, due to the unavoidable restrictions which safeguard the babies," cameraman Clark wrote. "They are allowed no more time before our cameras than when they were babies. One hour a day from 11 a.m. until noon. Since the next item on their daily schedule is lunch, twelve o'clock was very positively the end of our shooting day with the children. Nothing could interfere with that! The intensity of light to which the quints can be subjected is also strictly limited... [The lights] were regularly diffused with a daylight-blue gelatin and a silk... With only six [lights] to work with, and those diffused to the maximum of softness, the only type of lighting possible is a very simple, balanced lighting. As a rule, I used the daylight coming through the windows for my key light, and balanced the artificial light to that key. It was also necessary to spread my illumination over a rather broad angle, so that we might be ready to take advantage of any unexpected action by any of the five youngsters, no matter where it took place."

THE QUINTS AND JEAN HERSHOLT IN THE BACKYARD OF THE
DAFOE HOSPITAL WHILE FILMING *FIVE OF A KIND*.

"Each night, director Leeds and I would carefully plan the next day's work," Clark continued. "When 11 o'clock came the next morning, we would have everything set up, camera and sound equipment ready, and lights on while we, thoroughly disinfected and clad in surgical robes, caps and masks, awaited our five little actresses."

The Fox employees included LeVaughn Larson, who was in charge of the Quints' costumes. Due to Dafoe's strict health code, the actual dressing was performed by the girls' regular nurses. These nurses also performed the daily ritual of using their fingers to curl the sisters' naturally straight hair into Shirley Temple-like locks, not only for the movie and still cameras but also for the daily exhibitions in the playground. The curls enraged Elzire Dionne, who wanted her daughters' hair kept in its natural condition. Although the identical girls each wore a hair ribbon with an individual color, this device didn't help movie audiences to tell them apart since the picture was in black and white.

"When the weather permitted," Clark recalled, "we did our filming outdoors, in the children's playyard [sic]. For this reflectors were of course taboo. An adult finds it hard enough to face a battery of reflectors; they would be unbearable to children's eyes."

The Quints' exterior scenes in *Five of a Kind* included a charming candid moment in which Hersholt presents them with a quintet of cocker spaniel puppies. The surprised girls had never seen live dogs before, and their authentic facial expressions are delightful. "To the little ones [moviemaking] was play. Play with 'Monsieur le camera,' as they called it," Hersholt said. "Never have I had so much fun with the quints as on this last visit. Never have I seen them so lively, so full of pep, so beautiful, so delightfully mischievous...They are the most imitative little rascals imaginable...They are the happiest children I have ever seen. In all my visits to Callender [sic] I have never seen them crying, except once when one of them cried for a few seconds." Even off-camera, Hersholt's little co-stars called him "Doctor." "He had a broad, kindly smile," the quintuplets recalled many years later. "We enjoyed his company."

The shooting of a scene where the girls perform on toy pianos took place during one of their daily public exhibitions, forcing the crew to post a large sign that read: "Please co-operate [sic]. Silence is requested." For some shots, the cameras were concealed to prevent the Quints from being distracted and staring into the lenses.

JEAN HERSHOLT AND THE DIONNE QUINTUPLETS IN THEIR THIRD
FEATURE TOGETHER, *FIVE OF A KIND*.

"Many days," Clark wrote, "when we had planned to work outdoors, the weather turned cloudy, and we had to transpose our scenes indoors. In many ways, this proved an advantage, however, for it gave us an opportunity to show many rooms in the hospital which had never before been shown in motion pictures. We have scenes not only in the yard and the quints' playroom, but in their bedroom, dining room, and so on. Working in some of these rooms was a problem, for the largest, the playroom, measures but 17 by 20 feet, and the others are proportionately smaller. Nonetheless, in spite of all these difficulties, we worked fast. One day, in our short one-hour working time, we made as many as 26 set-ups! Careful planning was naturally the secret of the success."

Unlike *The Country Doctor* and *Reunion,* which both utilized extensive post-dubbing for the Quints' scenes, all of the girls' footage in *Five of a Kind* appears to use the actual sounds that were recorded on the set. The screenplay, which noted that "The Quints' lines can be dubbed if necessary," had provided more dialogue for the girls than ended up in the movie. The sisters probably had no trouble delivering their one line of dialogue, "Hello, Dr. Luke," since "doctor" was the first word that they had learned to speak. The

limited communication between Hersholt and the Quints in the film is real-
istic. There was very little verbal interaction between Dafoe and the Quints
since the doctor couldn't speak French and the girls couldn't speak English.

"At work, most of the communication between members of the crew had
to be by pantomime, in a set of carefully arranged signals," Clark recalled.
"This was necessary, not only because we were shooting everything in sound,
but so as to avoid distracting the attention of our young players. This time,
too, our shooting was far less a matter of chance of taking whatever the
quints chose to do and hoping for the best than ever before. As four-year-
olds they have now grown old enough to understand when they are told to
do definite things. Thus each has very specific 'business' to do, and to some
extent definite lines to speak…As a result, we are going to be able to use far
more footage of the quintuplets in this picture than in either of the two previous ones. Before, their scenes were more or less incidental, and their total
released footage did not exceed 750 feet. In this picture, their scenes are dra-

JOHN QUALEN (LEFT) AND SLIM SUMMERVILLE (MIDDLE) PROVIDED
COMIC RELIEF ONE AGAIN IN *FIVE OF A KIND*, THEIR THIRD QUINT
FEATURE. CESAR ROMERO WAS THE ROMANTIC LEAD.

matically important to the story, and we expect to use more than 2500 feet of quint scenes." (*Five of a Kind* was Clark's final feature. He concentrated on the technical aspects of cinematography and won a special Oscar in 1943 for developing a lens calibration system.)

Appearing briefly, silently, and unbilled in the picture were real-life Quint nurses Mollie O'Shaughnessey (also in *Reunion*), Sigrid Ulrichson and Louise Corriveau. (They were also featured in the Quints' short subjects.) When Wurtzel learned that the nurses' involvement in *Five of a Kind* was invaluable, he authorized a $50 bonus for each of them.

The Fox company returned to California in late June to complete the filming, which continued on the lot until late July.

Cast as the reporters were Fox contract players Claire Trevor and Cesar Romero. Trevor had been in more than two dozen pictures since 1933, most notably *Dante's Inferno* (1935), *Dead End* (1937), and *The Amazing Dr. Clitterhouse* (1938). Latin actor Romero had made his movie debut the same year as Trevor, and his extensive credits included *The Thin Man* (1934), *The Devil Is a Woman* (1935) with Marlene Dietrich, *Wee Willie Winkie* (1937) with Shirley Temple, and *Happy Landing* (1938) with Sonia Henie. Trevor and Romero had already worked for Wurtzel in "B" pictures, including *15 Maiden Lane* (1936), a detective picture that they co-starred in. Trevor and Romero were the two best actors to play romantic leads in a Quint feature, but the material doesn't serve them well and there is no chemistry between them.

Originally announced as Trevor's wisecracking sidekick was Joan Davis, an excellent verbal and physical comic previously used to good advantage in the studio's *Thin Ice* (1937) and *Life Begins in College* (1937). Unfortunately, Davis was replaced by Inez Courtney, a minor performer (*The Captain Hates the Sea* [1934], *The Hurricane* [1937]), who wasn't able to rise above the lame verbal and slapstick material in *Five of a Kind*.

Back for more comic relief was Slim Summerville and John Qualen. Qualen is seen operating a gift shop like the real Papa Dionne's, and his character is again concerned that the birth of sextuplets will overshadow his own girls' fame. Papa's fertility is again used as a source of humor. After hitting a dartboard's bull's-eye five times in a row, he boasts to the constable, "It ain't luck, it's technique." (As in *Reunion,* the mother isn't seen or discussed.) Hersholt, Qualen, and Summerville's weak scenes in this entry seem as tacked on as the Quints' segments. Because Fox never sent Qualen on any of the Callander trips, Papa Wyatt has no interaction with his quintuplets in any of the three features.

JEAN HERSHOLT, CLAIRE TREVOR, AND INEZ COURTNEY IN
FIVE OF A KIND.

In *Five of a Kind*, the Sir Basil Crawford character played by Montagu
Love in the first two pictures is no longer comedic and is played this time by
David Torrence, who had portrayed another political figure in *The Country
Doctor*. Jane Darwell returned to the series as a kindly nurse, but with a dif-
ferent name and at a different hospital than in *The Country Doctor*.

At $500,000 (including the Quints' $100,000 fee), the picture was far
costlier than a typical Fox "B" production, which rarely exceeded $200,000.
With the picture not scheduled for release until late October, *Five of a Kind*
had the least-rushed post-production of the three Quintuplets features.

Fox previewed the picture at the Alexander Theater in Glendale, California on October 7, 1938, where the sneak was well received by audience and
press. *Motion Picture Herald* reported: "Every minute of [the Quints'] appearance found the audience on the alert…Every time the little girls moved onto
the screen, [the audience] was attentive and appreciative." *The Exhibitor* predicted: "Should easily top draw of *Country Doctor*," while *The Hollywood Reporter* called the picture "A natural for big box office. Worth five times the
entrance fee."

The girls first show up fifteen minutes into *Five of a Kind,* when five-year-old actor Johnny Russell arrives to give Dr. Luke a basket of puppies for the Wyatt Quintuplets. (Rear-screen projection is used for a brief shot showing Russell with the stars.) To explain the Quints' strange noises to Russell (and to American audiences), Hersholt tells the boy, "They're speaking French, but they're learning English, too." (The statement turned out to be wishful thinking on Fox's part.)

At various points in the 85-minute feature, the Quints are seen bathing their dolls and putting them to bed, playing on rocking horses, frolicking on a hammock, and having a tea party with Hersholt. A cute highlight is when the tots are at first frightened, then amused, by a creepy Jack-in-the-Box during the climactic birthday party.

Appearing in a quintet of scenes for a total of twenty minutes, the girls are in more footage in *Five of a Kind* than in *The Country Doctor* and *Reunion* combined. (The Quints' screen time is even longer if you include the different stills of them that are seen throughout the feature in newspaper ads, a billboard, and a poster.) Some of this footage is presented as excerpts from a Fox-Movietone newsreel, despite the fact that the rival Pathe had exclusive

JEAN HERSHOLT, CLAIRE TREVOR, AND INEZ COURTNEY IN
FIVE OF A KIND.

FLYER FROM THE BROAD THEATER IN PENNSGROVE, PA.

newsreel rights. In reality, the Quints may have been distinct and different, but, despite Trevor's dialogue describing them as "alike as peas in a pod, yet each with an individual personality," it is impossible to tell the precious girls apart in *Five of a Kind*.

Although the Dionne Quintuplets are adorable, photogenic, and blessed with charisma, they do not display any true talents in the two sequences where they actually "perform." During their rendition of the children's song, "Frere Jacques" (which briefly uses rear-screen projection to create the illusion that Trevor is in the same location), the little girls lose interest and barely finish the tune. But it is the Quints' performance of the specialty song, "All Mixed Up," which was designed as the movie's highlight, that proves why they were not destined to be Fox's replacement for the maturing Shirley Temple. During the routine, which takes up the entire final six minutes of the feature, the five tots try vainly to remember the foreign words that they had learned phonetically and constantly look off camera at their teacher as they mimic some simple gestures. The number concludes with the sisters doing an elementary dance before curtsying for the fade-out.

In the *Five of a Kind* opening credits, the Quints' received their best billing yet; a single card reading "The Dionne Quintuplets," followed by superimposed close-ups of each girl with their first name appearing underneath. (Again, Dafoe's credit for his "supervision" was larger than the supporting cast's billing.) Fox's advertising material, playing up the musical sequences, screamed "Real entertainers now! Each a different personality! Singing, dancing, talking, trouping!" For once, all of the Quint photos used in the promotional materials were actually from the film.

On October 11, 1938, Hersholt arrived at Grauman's Chinese Theater in Hollywood for a special ceremony. In addition to placing his handprints, footprints, and pipe print into a square of wet cement, the actor also imprinted five pairs of shoes that the Quints had worn in *Five of a Kind*. Hersholt autographed the cement and also wrote "Yvonne," "Annette," "Cecile," "Emilie," and "Marie" under the tiny shoe imprints. Unfortunately, the square didn't last any longer than the Quints' movie careers. Within weeks, the poorly prepared cement block started to crumble and was soon replaced by a blank slab.

As usual, fan magazines, such as *Modern Movies, Silver Screen* and *Screen Romances,* carried stories on the new movie. The October 11 issue of *Look* featured an NEA photo of Dafoe and the Quints on the cover, but the magazine apparently balked at paying the extra fee required to publish movie stills of the Quints. Inside the magazine, the *Five of a Kind* costumes were modeled by child actor Mila Samrich (*Stella Dallas,* [1937]) instead of by the stars themselves.

Although official Dionne Quintuplet dolls could be glimpsed in the background during the picture's final scene, dolls were not sold in theater lobbies this time, and movie tie-in doll outfits were not created. The only *Five of a Kind* tie-in was "All Mixed Up" sheet music featuring a photo of the Quints in the "Swiss Miss" costumes on the cover. The song was not a hit, but the curious few who bought it could read the lyrics and find out what the girls had been trying to sing in the picture.

The movie opened in California and New York in late October 1938. One movie house in Deposit, New York held a special matinee showing where four-year-old girls received free admission, cake, ice cream, and gifts. ("Your Birth Certificate is Your Admission.")

Five of a Kind received the poorest reviews of the girls' three features. *Variety* reported: "As third of the Dionne Quint features, *Five of a Kind* will find difficulty in generating much audience enthusiasm except in spots where women patronage predominates. Picture has been strung together on a hokey and slapsticky framework that has many dull moments and situations…Youngsters are at the cute age that is granted but repetition of their appearances in the picture to do nothing more than the same cute tricks that all four-year-olds perform for doting parents and friends gets monotonous. Without training to perform in unison, for presentation of either songs or dances, Quints consume entirely too much footage. Extemporaneous antics of the youngsters are paraded to extreme…Background story is not a particularly good showcase for the Quints. Yarn is lightly strung together and full of obvious situations that fail to sustain interest…Switches in tempo during the unfolding are numerous."

The equally unimpressed Frank S. Nugent of *The New York Times* said: "[The girls] sing a few off-key ditties and dance a pleasantly clumsy minuet. They all have big feet. It may be ironic justice that the quins [sic] have become, in their latest film, the victims of mass production. *Five of a Kind* is an obviously factory-made product, with a synthetically superimposed plot… and not a trace of the humor which relieved the two earlier Dionne films. The test of a Dionne picture should not be whether the children are cute to watch (any quintet of 4-year-olds is bound to be), but whether it has any value apart from their presence. This one has none."

"[The Dionne Quintuplets] give no impression of taking their profession seriously," complained a sarcastic reviewer for *Time*. "In the first place none of the quintuplets has bothered to learn English. In the second place, what they speak, although it sounds vaguely like French, is really some sort of

THE DIONNE QUINTUPLETS PERFORM THEIR BIG SONG AND DANCE NUMBER IN THE FINALE OF *FIVE OF A KIND*. NOTE THE OFFICIAL QUINT DOLLS IN THE BACKGROUND.

squirrel talk, whose complete unintelligibility to outsiders appears to delight rather than distress the Dionnes...When they are called upon to render the simple little nursery ballad, *Frere Jacques*, [they] are so impudent as to sing it in five different keys, squealing and chuckling as they do so."

Once again, the public paid no attention to the bad reviews. *Five of a Kind* sold $1 million worth of tickets and was Fox's ninth highest grossing film of 1938. (The continued success of the three features is surprising since the Quint footage in the Pathe newsreels was always much more interesting, varied, and extensive.) But Quintmania was running out of steam.

✦ The Quintuplets Retire from Show Business

Early in 1938, the girls' fourth birthday didn't receive the same amount of publicity as their previous ones. Madame Alexander's Quint dolls were still available in stores, but no new styles of either the dolls or their outfits were issued. The once-ubiquitous Dionne Quintuplet merchandise and product endorsement also began to decrease.

The 1939 Pathe short, *Five Times Five*, showed the girls celebrating their fifth birthday and included footage of the Quints kissing the ring of His Excellency Bishop Nelligan and pulling off his cap. The movie was nominated for an Academy Award for Best Two-Reel Short Subject, but it didn't boost the girls' movie careers.

Public and promotional interest in the Quints continued to decline throughout 1939, and, a short time later, when World War II began, the tourist trade suffered due partly to the rationing of tires and gas. Also affected was the Quints' exclusive still-photo deal. NEA could no longer sell the photos to the European market, and the American papers were more interested in printing war-related images.

Because *The Country Doctor*, *Reunion*, and *Five of a Kind* had all been made on relatively low budgets and had paid off at the box office, Zanuck was still interested in making a fourth movie starring the girls. But he had second thoughts when he considered the public's declining interest in the Quints and the hefty fees and percentages demanded by the guardians. He knew that story ideas would once again be limited by the guardians' refusal to let the stars be filmed outside the Dafoe Hospital and by the girls' limited performing skills. But it was the Dionne parents' refusal to let the Quints learn English that concerned the studio the most. Realizing that you could only sustain a gimmick for so long, Zanuck dropped Fox's option for a fourth Dionne Quintuplets feature.

In 1940 the girls were guests on the radio show *Ontario Night,* but their inability to speak English killed their chance for substantial radio success. The Quints' popularity decreased, but the tensions between the girls' father and the guardians continued to increase. After a long and bitter legal struggle, Oliva Dionne gained control of his famous daughters, and the eight-year-old Quints were removed from the Dafoe Hospital in 1942. The following year, Dr. Dafoe, whose name and image had become as ubiquitous as those of the Quints, died of pneumonia.

The Dionne Quintuplets now lived with their parents and seven other siblings in a huge new house that had been paid for with money from the Quints' trust fund. "My managers and myself would…accept a moving picture occasionally and the use of the name 'Dionne Quintuplets' for a few high-class articles," Oliva Dionne told the press. But the former movie stars never appeared in another fictional motion picture. The Quints later recalled: "At the back of his mind, Dad nursed the thought of keeping us in the public eye and somehow getting us back into movies…[H]e stage-managed what he possibly hoped would be the start of a career for us as entertainers. We were constantly being taught songs and drills and dances by the nuns who were our teachers…[Dad] has said never a word to us about *The Country Doctor* … Nor has he mentioned any of the other movies we appeared in."

Pathe allowed its exclusive newsreel rights to expire, and the Quints' few public appearances in the 1940s and '50s were recorded by numerous newsreel companies, including Fox-Movietone. The daily exhibitions of the Dionne Quintuplets ended when the girls were ten. Except for a few uncomfortable appearances at Victory Bond rallies when the girls were preteens, their careers as entertainers were over. The only piece of Dionne Quintuplet merchandise that was still available was a popular calendar that continued until 1955. Each calendar featured a different painting that looked nothing like the real-life Quints.

As the Dionne Quintuplets grew into awkward teenagers and troubled adults, they retreated from the public eye. None of the sisters had any interest in performing. Yvonne, Annette, Cecile, Emilie, and Marie each went on to live an unhappy life. The earnings of the former child movie stars were mismanaged, and they were not financially rewarded for the millions of dollars that they had generated in the 1930s. Emilie died of suffocation during an epileptic seizure in 1954, Marie of a blood clot in the brain in 1970, and

Yvonne of cancer in 2001. Annette and Cecile, the two surviving but ailing Quints, live together in Canada.

The Country Doctor, Reunion, and *Five of a Kind* were never re-released for a second theatrical run, but were syndicated to television in the mid-1950s by National Telefilm Associates in a package with several hundred other pre-1948 Twentieth Century-Fox movies. In 1963 the Dionne Quintuplets wrote: "Sometimes late at night on television, there are the old movies of five little girls in identical clothes with identical smiles and identical curls. It seems that they could not possibly be us but some rare, legendary children from an age of innocence, saved for always from growing up."

The three features of the Dionne Quintuplets are not lost films (a complete print of each is held at UCLA's Film and Television Archive), but they have not been shown on television in decades, have never been released on home video, and have become as elusive and obscure as the stars themselves. A TV or home video release is very unlikely due to the films' curio status and obscurity. To see the features, diehard Dionne Quintuplets fans and curious movie buffs have had to track down poor-quality "collectors' market" VHS and DVD copies made from battered 16mm TV prints. (Clips from the movies have been shown at the Callander Bay Heritage Museum, which is housed in the former home of Dr. Dafoe.) Memorabilia related to the features (posters, lobby cards, etc.) and prints of the home movies are highly priced and actively sought after by the many Quint collectors.

The three features of the Dionne Quintuplets are not film classics, and today they are little more than Golden Age curiosities, but the films are captivating and entertaining records of a time when five little miracle babies, who were never even required to act, became the highest-paid movie stars of the era and provided pleasant escapism to millions of moviegoers.

✦ Filmography

NOTE: In addition to the Pathe-produced documentary shorts listed below, the Dionne Quintuplets also appeared in segments of Pathe Newsreels throughout the 1930s.

A Day in the Lives of the Dionne Quintuplets (1934) (Short Subject)

CAST:
> The Dionne Quintuplets (Yvonne, Cecile, Marie, Annette, Emilie), Dr. Allan R. Dafoe.

PRODUCTION CREDITS:
> Director: Claude Collins. Photography: Roy Tash.
> Produced by Pathe. Distributed by RKO Radio Pictures. Production date: October 19, 1934. Sound. Black & White. 1 Reel. Running time (approximately): 10 minutes.

The Dionne Quintuplets at Play (1935) (Short Subject)

CAST:
> The Dionne Quintuplets (Yvonne, Cecile, Marie, Annette, Emilie), Dr. Allan R. Dafoe.

PRODUCTION CREDITS:
> Director: Claude Collins. Photography: Roy Tash.
> Produced by Pathe. Distributed by RKO Radio Pictures. Sound. Black & White. 2 reels. Running time (approximately): 16 minutes.

The Quintuplets' Second Christmas (1935) (Short Subject)

CAST:
>   The Dionne Quintuplets (Yvonne, Cecile, Marie, Annette, Emilie), Dr. Allan R. Dafoe.

PRODUCTION CREDITS:
>   Director: Claude Collins. Photography: Roy Tash.
>   Produced by Pathe. Distributed by RKO Radio Pictures. Sound. Black & White. 2 reels. Running time (approximately): 16 minutes.

The Country Doctor (1936) (Feature Film)

CAST:
>   The Dionne Quintuplets: Yvonne, Cecile, Marie, Annette, Emilie (The Wyatt Quintuplets), Jean Hersholt (Dr. John Luke), June Lang (Mary MacKenzie), Slim Summerville (Constable Jim Ogden), Michael Whalen (Tony Luke), Dorothy Peterson (Nurse Katherine Kennedy), Robert Barrat ("Mac" MacKenzie), John Qualen (Asa Wyatt), Montagu Love (Sir Basil Crawford), Jane Darwell (Mrs. Graham), Frank Reicher (Dr. Paul Luke), David Torrence (Governor General), George Chandler (Greasy), Helen Jerome Eddy (Mrs. Ogden), Aileen Carlyle (Mrs.Wyatt), George Meeker (Dr. Wilson), J. Anthony Hughes (Mike), William Benedict (The Gawker), Harry Cording (Lumberjack), Wilfred Lucas (Proprietor), Richard Carlyle (Bishop) (uncredited), Mary Carr (Woman) (uncredited), William Conlon (Peg-leg Walter) (uncredited), John Dilson (City Editor) (uncredited), Margaret Fielding (Secretary) (uncredited), Claude King (Toastmaster) (uncredited), Paul McVey (Mack) (uncredited), Edward McWade (Editor) (uncredited), Dillon Ober (Piano player) (uncredited), Garry Owen (Jerry) (uncredited), Kane Richmond (Logger) (uncredited), Florence Roberts (Grandmother) (uncredited), Joe Sawyer (Joe) (uncredited), Delmar Watson (Boy) (uncredited), Cecil Weston (Woman) (uncredited), Harry C. Bradley (uncredited), Tom Kennedy (uncredited), Monte Vandegrift (uncredited), Bill Conlin (uncredited), Pat Flaherty (uncredited), Jeanne Hart (uncredited), Barlowe Borland (uncredited), Harry Harvey (uncredited), Thomas Pogue (uncredited)

PRODUCTION CREDITS:

Director: Henry King. Producer: Darryl F. Zanuck (uncredited). Associate Producer: Nunnally Johnson. Screenplay: Sonya Levien [and Nunnally Johnson (uncredited)]. Story idea suggested by Charles E. Blake. Music Director: Louis Silvers. Photography: John Seitz, A.S.C., Daniel B. Clark, A.S.C. Art Direction: Mark-Lee Kirk. Sets: Thomas Little. Assistant Director: Robert Webb. Film Editing: Barbara McLean. Costumes: Gwen Wakeling. Technical Supervision for scenes of the Dionne Quintuplets: Dr. Allan R. Dafoe. Sound: Bernard Freericks, Roger Heman. Business Executive for Twentieth Century-Fox: Joseph Moskowitz (uncredited). Artistic Director of Effects: Philip De Esco (uncredited). Assistant Editors: Robert Fritch (uncredited), Richard Billings (uncredited). Publicity: Frank Perrett (uncredited), Harry Brand (uncredited). Stunt Pilot: Paul Mantz (uncredited).

Produced and Distributed by Twentieth Century-Fox Film Corporation. Production dates: December 4, 1935 late January 1936. Released March 4, 1936. Copyright date: March 6, 1936. Sound (Western Electric Noiseless Recording). Black & White. 10 reels, 8,680 ft. Running time: 94 minutes.

SYNOPSIS:

Dedicated country doctor John Luke serves in Moosetown, a small rural community in northern Canada. Dr. Luke and his faithful nurse, Katherine Kennedy, spend most of their time treating injured lumberjacks. Dr. Luke refuses payment from most patients. Dr. Luke goes to the home of Asa Wyatt and his wife to deliver the couple's seventh child. During the freezing winter, many children fatally fall victim to a diphtheria epidemic. Due to the weather and loss of communication, Dr. Luke is unable to receive diphtheria serum. Nurse Kennedy is distraught at her inability to save the children. Dr. Luke finally is able to radio his brother, Dr. Paul Luke, in Montreal. Dr. Luke's brother and Dr. Luke's nephew, Tony, visit Sir Basil Crawford, the pompous leader of the logging company and ask him to send a plane with medical supplies to Moosetown. When Crawford refuses, Tony flies a plane himself, accompanied by Greasy. Tony and Greasy arrive with the serum, but the plane is damaged and they are stranded in Moosetown until the spring. Mary's father, "Mac" MacKenzie, the temperamental district manager, is angry about Mary's budding relationship with Tony and about her working for Dr. Luke as a nurse. In the spring, Dr. Luke travels to Montreal to request funding for a proper Moosetown hospital, but is unsuccessful at obtaining a meeting with Crawford. Dr. Luke goes to a dinner party where Crawford is in attendance. He describes the poor medical conditions in Moosetown and publicly pleads with Crawford to fund a hospital. Tony was planning to return to Montreal to continue his medical studies, but he is forced to stay in Moosetown when the enraged MacKenzie damages the plane. Tony proposes to Mary shortly before he breaks her father's arm in a tavern brawl. Constable Jim Ogden tries to arrest Tony, but Tony flies off, stranding Greasy once again. Crawford sends another doctor to Moosetown to replace Dr. Luke, much to MacKenzie's approval. MacKenzie tells the loggers to shun Dr. Luke. Nurse Kennedy pleads with Dr. Luke to leave Moosetown and accept a job at his brother's hospital. MacKenzie discovers that Dr. Luke does not have a medical license. Dr. Luke admits that, while he graduated from medical school, he never bothered applying for a license. Constable Ogden reluctantly orders Dr. Luke to leave Moosetown. As Dr. Luke boards the boat, Asa Wyatt arrives and begs the doctor to deliver his new baby. Nurse Kennedy, Asa, and Constable Ogden assist as Dr. Luke makes medical history by miraculously delivering five tiny baby girls. The world is stunned at the birth of the first surviving quintuplets in history. Swarms of reporters and tourists arrive to see the famous Wyatt Quintuplets: Yvonne, Cecile, Marie, Annette, and Emilie. Greasy organizes tours of the area. Constable Ogden gives interviews to the press. Dr. Luke modestly shuns the praise and turns down lucrative product endorsements. Nurse Kennedy and Dr. Luke adore the babies and love to care for and play with them. Even the gruff MacKenzie is won over by the charming quintuplets. Mary is delighted when Tony arrives back in town. MacKenzie tells Constable Ogden to tear up Tony's arrest warrant. The following year Crawford and the general governor arrive to dedicate a new hospital and to present Dr. Luke with the Order of the British Empire.

Going on Two (1936) (Short Subject)

CAST:
The Dionne Quintuplets (Yvonne, Cecile, Marie, Annette, Emilie), Dr. Allan R. Dafoe.

PRODUCTION CREDITS:
Director: Claude Collins. Photography: Roy Tash.
Produced by Pathe. Distributed by RKO Radio Pictures. Sound. Black & White. 2 reels. Running time (approximately): 16 minutes.

Reunion (1936) (Feature Film)

CAST:
The Dionne Quintuplets: Yvonne, Cecile, Marie, Annette, Emilie (The Wyatt Quintuplets), Jean Hersholt (Dr. John Luke), Rochelle Hudson (Mary MacKenzie), Helen Vinson (Gloria Sheridan), Slim Summerville (Constable Jim Ogden), Robert Kent (Tony Luke), John Qualen (Asa Wyatt), Dorothy Peterson (Nurse Katherine Kennedy), Alan Dinehart (Philip Crandell), J. Edward Bromberg (Charles Renard), Sara Haden (Ellie), Montagu Love (Sir Basil Crawford), Tom Moore (Dr. Richard Sheridan), George Ernest (Rusty), Esther Ralston (Janet Fair), Katherine Alexander (Mrs. Crandall), Julius Tannen (Sam Fisher), George Chandler (Harry, the Crook), Edward McWade (Editor), Maude Eburne (Mrs. Barton), Claudia Coleman (Mrs. Simms), Hank Mann (Jake), Hattie McDaniel (Sadie), Arthur S. "Pop" Byron (Prison Guard) (uncredited), Eddie Dunn (Gardener) (uncredited), Grace Hayle (Mrs. Williams) (uncredited), Joan Howard (Baby Williams) (uncredited), Mary MacLaren (Mrs. Ogden) (uncredited), Colonel McDonnell (Guardsman) (uncredited), Yvonne Leroux (Nurse) (uncredited), Jacqueline Noel (Nurse) (uncredited), Mollie O'Shaughnessey (Nurse) (uncredited), Henry Roquemore (Bald-headed Man) (uncredited), Adrian Rosley (Band Leader) (uncredited), Mickey Rentschler (Boy) (uncredited), Buster Slaven (Boy) (uncredited), Billy Mahan (Kid with Mallet) (uncredited), Jim Toney (uncredited).

PRODUCTION CREDITS:
Director: Norman Taurog. In Charge of Production: Darryl F. Zanuck. Associate Producers: Earl Carroll, Harold Wilson, Bogart Rogers (all uncredited). Screenplay: Sam Hellman, Gladys Lehman, Sonya Levien [and Walter Ferris (uncredited).] Story: Bruce Gould. Special sequences written by Jack Mintz (uncredited). Photography: Daniel B. Clark, A.S.C. Art Direction: Mark-Lee Kirk. Set Decorations: Thomas Little. Assistant Director: Ed O'Fearna. Film Editor: Jack Murray. Costumes: [Luis] Royer. Sound: W.D. Flick, Roger Heman. Musical Direction: Emil Newman. Technical Supervision for scenes of the Dionne Quintuplets: Dr. Allan R. Dafoe. Wardrobe: Arthur Levy (uncredited), Ollie Hughes (uncredited). Music by David Buttolph. (uncredited), Cyril J. Mockridge (uncredited). Publicity: Harry Brand (uncredited). Props: Joe Behm (uncredited), Frank Sullivan (uncredited).Generator Man: Bill Russell (uncredited).

Produced and Distributed by Twentieth Century-Fox Film Corporation. Production dates: August 17, 1936- late October 1936. Released November 27, 1936. Copyright date: November 20, 1936. Sound (Western Electric Noiseless Recording). Black & White. 8 reels, 7,235 ft. Running time: 81 minutes.

SYNOPSIS:
Dr. John Luke, the country doctor in the Canadian town of Moosetown, who is famous worldwide for delivering the Wyatt Quintuplets, delivers his 3,000[th] baby. Dr. Luke plans to retire and reluctantly agrees to the town leaders' plans to throw a huge reunion party for all of the people that were delivered by him. Among those invited is Governor Phillip Crandall, the first baby delivered by Dr. Luke, who plans to attend with his wife, Martha. Also invited is faded, disillusioned movie star Janet Fair. When Janet receives the lead in a New York show, her manager urges her to attend the reunion for publicity. Dr. Luke and nurse Mary MacKenzie treat the bruised knuckles of Rusty, a boy who had been taunted about being an orphan. Mary is excited that Dr. Luke's nephew, Tony, is coming to succeed Dr. Luke as the Moosetown doctor. At Dr. Luke's Hospital for the Quintuplets, Dr. Luke checks in with Nurse Katherine Kennedy and watches the two-year-old quintuplets Yvonne, Cecile, Marie, Annette, and Emi-

lie at play. Constable Jim Ogden believes that his wife is going to deliver sextuplets and Asa Wyatt, father of the quintuplets, is concerned about being upstaged. To Asa's delight, Mrs. Ogden gives birth to only one baby. Thousands arrive for the reunion party. Town council member Charles Renard has secretly loved Janet since childhood and is excited by her arrival. Bank robber Harry escapes from jail to attend the party and to pick pockets. Crandall develops a fatherly affection for Rusty. Dr. Luke insinuates that Crandall may be the boy's real father. Tony's mentor, Dr. Richard Sheridan, and his decades-younger wife, Gloria, arrive. Dr. Luke and Mary learn that Tony is having an affair with Gloria. Gloria tells Tony that she plans to divorce her husband to be with Tony. Dr. Luke berates the ashamed Tony about the affair. Dr. Sheridan tells Dr. Luke that he suspects that Gloria is seeing another man. Dr. Luke tells Gloria that Tony loves Mary and not her and that she should stay with her husband. Dr. Luke arranges for Gloria to overhear Tony admit that he loves Mary and not Gloria. A huge outdoor luncheon is served and politician Sir Basil Crawford announces Dr. Luke, who gives a modest speech. To the delight of the massive crowd, the Wyatt Quintuplets arrive at the party in five horse-drawn carriages and frolic in the playground. Asa is disappointed that he is not introduced at the luncheon and has to climb a pole to get a glimpse at his own children. Dr. Sheridan and Gloria plan a second honeymoon. Janet shoots herself with a pistol when she receives a telegram telling her that she is no longer wanted for the New York show. With Mary's assistance, Tony operates on and saves Janet. Renard waits by Janet's bedside. Constable Ogden takes the stolen items from Harry and tells the pickpocket to return to prison. Constable Ogden's dog has sextuplets in the back of Crawford's car. Tony and Mary reunite and make a house call to deliver a baby. Asa fears that they will deliver sextuplets. Crandall and Martha adopt Rusty.

A Day at Home (1937) (Short Subject)

CAST:

The Dionne Quintuplets (Yvonne, Cecile, Marie, Annette, Emilie), Dr. Allan R. Dafoe.

PRODUCTION CREDITS:
Director: Claude Collins. Photography: Roy Tash.
Produced by Pathe. Distributed by RKO Radio Pictures. Sound.
Black & White. 2 reels. Running time (approximately): 16 minutes.
(This short was also released to the 16mm and 8mm home movie
market in late 1937 by Pathegrams, Inc., the home movie division of
Pathe, in a complete 350-foot 16mm sound version and in con-
densed 16mm silent versions of 25 feet, 50 feet, 100 feet and 350 feet
and in condensed 8mm silent versions of 50 feet and 175 feet.)

A Day with the Dionne Quints (1937) (Short Subject)

CAST:
The Dionne Quintuplets (Yvonne, Cecile, Marie, Annette, Emilie),
Dr. Allan R. Dafoe.

PRODUCTION CREDITS:
Director: Claude Collins. Photography: Roy Tash.
Produced by Pathe. Distributed by RKO Radio Pictures. Sound.
Black & White. 2 reels. Running time (approximately): 16 minutes.

Quintupland (1938) (Short Subject)

CAST:
The Dionne Quintuplets (billed as The Dionne Darlings) (Yvonne,
Cecile, Marie, Annette, Emilie), Dr. Allan R. Dafoe.
PRODUCTION CREDITS:
Director: Claude Collins. Photography: Roy Tash.
Produced by Pathe. Distributed by RKO Radio Pictures. Sound.
Black & White. 2 reels. Running time (approximately): 16 minutes.

Five of a Kind (1938) (Feature Film)

CAST:
The Dionne Quintuplets: Yvonne, Cecile, Marie, Annette, Emilie
(The Wyatt Quintuplets), Jean Hersholt (Dr. John Luke), Claire
Trevor (Christine Nelson), Cesar Romero (Duke Lester), Slim Sum-
merville (Constable Jim Ogden), Henry Wilcoxon (Dr. Scott Wil-
liams), Inez Courtney (Libby Long), John Qualen (Asa Wyatt), Jane
Darwell (Mrs. Waldron), Pauline Moore (Eleanor Kingsley), John

Russell (Dickie), Andrew Tombes (Dr. Bruno), David Torrence (Sir Basil Crawford), Marion Byron (Nurse Corday), Hamilton MacFadden (Andrew Gordon), Spencer Charters (Rev. Matthew Brand), Charles D. Brown (Editor Crane) (uncredited), Kay Griffith (Stewardess) (uncredited), Jack Norton (Drunk) (uncredited), Bert Roach (Big Man) (uncredited), Lester Dorr (Television Director) (uncredited), Claire Du Brey (Nurse) (uncredited), Esther Howard (Thelma) (uncredited), Ralph Dunn (Policeman) (uncredited), James Flavin (Policeman) (uncredited), John Collins (Man Standing on Head) (uncredited), Charles Tannen (Reporter) (uncredited), Syd Saylor (Truck Owner) (uncredited), Phyllis Fraser (Cashier) (uncredited), James Aubrey (Peddler) (uncredited), Ed Gargan (Writer) (uncredited), Eddie Anderson (Attendant) (uncredited), Charles Wilson (Editor Crocker) (uncredited), Lillian Porter (Phone Girl) (uncredited), Arthur Hoyt (Little Man), Val Brocker (Mme. Yukoff) (uncredited), Mollie O'Shaughnessey (Nurse) (uncredited), Sigrid Ulrichson (Nurse) (uncredited), Louise Corriveau (Nurse) (uncredited), Grace Hayle (uncredited), Ruth Warren (uncredited).

PRODUCTION CREDITS:

Director: Herbert I. Leeds. Executive Producer: Sol M. Wurtzel. In Charge of Production: Darryl F. Zanuck (uncredited). Original Screenplay: Lou Breslow, John Patrick. Photography: Daniel B. Clark, A.S.C. Art Direction: Bernard Herzbrun, Chester Gore. Set Decorations: Thomas Little. Film Editor: Fred Allen. Costume Design: Herschel [McCoy], Helen A. Myron. Sound: W. D. Flick, William H. Anderson. Song: "All Mixed Up" Words and Music by Sidney Clare and Samuel Pokrass. Musical Director: Samuel Kaylin. Technical Supervision for scenes of the Dionne Quintuplets: Dr. Allan R. Dafoe. Assistant Director: William Eckhardt (uncredited). Location Manager: R. C. Moore (uncredited). Business Executive for Twentieth Century-Fox: Joseph Moskowitz (uncredited). In Charge of Quintuplets' Dresses: LeVaughn Larson (uncredited). Props: Skippy Delfino (uncredited). Teacher and Nurse for the Dionne Quintuplets: Nora Rouselle (uncredited).

Produced and Distributed by Twentieth Century-Fox Film Corporation. Production dates: June 6, 1938 late July 1938. Released late October 1938. Copyright date: October 14, 1936. Sound (Western Electric Mirrophonic Recording). Black & White. 9 reels, 7,693 ft. Running time: 85 minutes.

Synopsis:

While covering the disappearance of heiress Elinor Kingsley, feisty New York newspaper reporter Christine Nelson stops at a house to make a phone call. Rival reporter Duke Lester enters the house with Miss Kingsley. Discovering that Claire is also a reporter, Duke feeds her a phony story about Miss Kingsley's fiancé being insane. When Claire's editor prints the story, the paper is sued and Claire is fired. Claire and her friend, Libby, go to the movies and see a newsreel featuring the famous, four-year-old Wyatt Quintuplets (Yvonne, Cecile, Marie, Annette, and Emilie) of Moosetown, Canada and their dedicated physician, Dr. John Luke. Claire begins hosting a radio show called *Newsreel of the Air*, which features offbeat personalities from around the world. Claire and Libby go to Moosetown to interview Dr. Luke and the quintuplets, but Duke arrives there first. Duke poses as a New York police inspector and tells Constable Jim Ogden and Asa Wyatt, father of the quintuplets, that Claire and Libby are wanted criminals. Constable Ogden arrests the women. Duke visits Dr. Luke and tries to get him to sign a contract granting him an exclusive radio interview with the quintuplets. When Dr. Luke and Constable Ogden discover Duke's deception, Duke flees back to the States. Claire's radio broadcast from Dr. Luke's Hospital for the Quintuplets captures the French-speaking Quintuplets playing pianos and singing "Frere Jacques." Back in New York, Claire rejects Duke's offer of friendship. Dr. Scott Williams requests that Claire organize a fund raiser with the quintuplets to raise money for an orphan's hospital. Claire gets the idea to have the quintuplets travel to New York for a live radio broadcast that would benefit the orphans. With the help of his shady friend, Dr. Bruno, Duke stages a fake sextuplet birth, which Claire covers on her radio show. When the hoax is exposed, the quintuplets' guardians distrust Claire and cancel the trip to New York. The guilt-stricken Duke visits Dr. Luke and Canadian politician Sir Basil Crawford and admits that Claire had nothing to do with the sextuplet fraud. The Quints' fourth birthday is broadcast to a huge audience at a New York theater via a "recently perfected television system." The broadcast shows the little girls singing and dancing. Claire learns that Duke organized the television presentation and they happily watch the show together.

Five Times Five (1939) (Short Subject)

Cast:

The Dionne Quintuplets (Yvonne, Cecile, Marie, Annette, Emilie), Dr. Allan R. Dafoe, His Excellency Bishop Nelligan.

PRODUCTION CREDITS:

Director: Claude Collins. Photography: Harry Smith. Editor: Jay Bonafield.

Produced by Pathe. Distributed by RKO Radio Pictures. Sound. Black & White. 2 Reels. Running time: 21 minutes.

Academy Award Nomination: Best Two-Reel Short, 1939.

✦ Bibliography

BOOKS:

John Axe, *The Collectible Dionne Quintuplets* (Riverdale, MD: Hobby House Press, 1977)

Lillian Barker, *The Dionne Legend: Quintuplets in Captivity* (Garden City, NY: Doubleday and Co., 1951)

Pierre Berton, *The Dionne Years: A Thirties Melodrama* (NY: W. W. Norton and Co., 1977)

W. E. Blatz, *Collected Studies on the Dionne Quintuplets* (Toronto: The University of Toronto Press, 1937)

James Brough with Annette, Cecile, Marie, and Yvonne Dionne, *We Were Five* (NY: Simon and Schuster, 1963)

Larry Ceplair, *A Great Lady: A Life of the Screenwriter Sonya Levien* (Lanham, MD and London: Scarecrow Press, Inc. 1996)

Walter Coppedge, *Henry King's America* (Metuchen, NJ and London: Scarecrow Press, 1986)

M. Louise Corriveau, *Quints to Queens* (NY: Vantage Press, 1976)

George F. Custen, *Twentieth Century's Fox: Darryl F. Zanuck and the Culture of Hollywood* (NY: Basic Books, 1997)

Dionne Quintuplets Play Mother Goose (NY: Dell Publishing Co., 1938)

Stacy Endres and Robert Cushman, *Hollywood at Your Feet: The Story of the World Famous Chinese Theater* (Los Angeles: Pomegranate Press, Ltd., 1992)

Raymond Fielding, *The American Newsreel 1911-1967* (Norman, OK: University of Oklahoma Press, 1972)

Mel Gussow, *Don't Say Yes Until I Finish Talking: A Biography of Darryl F. Zanuck* (Garden City, NY: Doubleday and Co., 1971)

Patricia King Hansen, editor, *The American Film Institute Catalog of Motion Pictures Produced in the United States: Feature Films, 1931-1940* (Berkeley: University of California Press, 1998)

Frazier Hunt, *The Little Doc: The Story of Allan Roy Dafoe* (NY: Simon and Schuster, 1939)

Ken Murray, *The Body Merchant: The Story of Earl Carroll* (Pasadena, CA: Ward Ritchie Press, 1976)

Aubrey Solomon, *Twentieth Century-Fox: A Corporate and Financial History* (Metuchen, NJ: Scarecrow Press, 1988)

Tom Stempel, *Screenwriter: The Life and Times of Nunnally Johnson* (San Diego: A. S. Barnes and Co., 1980)

Ellie Tesher, *The Dionnes* (Toronto: Doubleday, 1999)

Tony Thomas and Aubrey Solomon, *The Films of 20th Century-Fox* (Secaucus, NJ: Citadel Press, 1979)

Willis Thornton, *The Country Doctor* (NY: Grosset & Dunlap, 1936)

Dian Zillner, *Hollywood Collectibles* (West Chester, PA: Schiffer Publishing, Ltd., 1991)

ARTICLES:

Dora Albert, "Amazing Change in the Quintuplets," *Picture Play* (September 1938)

Charles E. Blake, "How They Got the Quints in Pictures," *Photoplay* (March 1936)

DeWitt Bodeen, "Rex Ingram and Alice Terry, Part One," *Films in Review* (Vol. XXVI No. 2) (February 1975)

Walter E. Burton, "Photographing the Dionne Quins," *Popular Science Monthly* (February 1937)

Daniel B. Clark. A.S.C., "Restrictions Hedge Quints When They Are Brought Before Camera," *American Cinematographer* (August 1938)

James Cunningham, "Quintuplets Do Their Own Script and Miles of Publicity for Fox," *Motion Picture Herald* (December 21, 1935)

Sam Hellman, Gladys Lehman, Sonya Levien, Bruce Gould, "The Dionne Quints' Second Picture," (condensed version of shooting script of *Reunion*), *Photoplay* (December 1936)

Jean Hersholt, "Five Little Stars," *Woman's Home Companion* (June 1939)

Sonia Lee, "What Two Stars Owe the Quints," *Movie Classic* (December 1936)

Chester Matthews, "Will They Be Radio Stars Tomorrow?" *Radio Guide* (April 25, 1936)

Keith Munro, "The Strange Case of the Dionne Quints," *Collier's* (April 23, 1949)

Marian Rhea, "Hollywood's White Hopes," *Movie Classic* (December 1936)

Howard Sharpe, "The Dionne Quintuplets and their Movie Money," *Movie Mirror* (September 1936)

Roy Tash, "Shooting the 'Quints,'" *The International Photographer* (December 1935)

Norman Taurog, "I'm a Fugitive From the Quints!" *Hollywood* (Vol. 26 No. 1) (January 1937)

"What the Quints Will Wear in Their New Picture," *Look* (October 11, 1938)

DOCUMENTARIES:

The Dionne Quintuplets (1978). National Film Board of Canada. Director/Producer: Donald Brittain.

Dionne Quintuplet Dolls: An Alexander Exclusive 1934-1939 (1992). Sirocco Productions, Inc. Director/Producer: Gayle O'Neal, Leonard Swann, Jr. Writer: Leonard Swann, Jr.

WEBSITES:

eBay (www.ebay.com)
Internet Movie Database (www.imdb.com)

Index

Bold italics indicates photo

A

Academy Award (Oscar), 16, 30, 38, 44, 73, 81
"All Mixed Up" (song), 65, 76, 77
Amazing Dr. Clitterhouse, The (film), 73
Ameche, Don, 52
American Cinematographer (magazine), 66
Arliss, George, 64

B

Baby LeRoy, 47, 48
Barrat, Robert, 28
Bedtime Story, A (1938 film), 47
Berton, Pierre, 9
Birth of a Nation, The (film), 31, 34
Blackley, Douglas, 51
Blake, Charlie, 15, 16, 17, 19, 20, 21, 26
Blatz, Dr. William, 59
Block, Paul, 34
Board of Guardians, 10, 11, 19, 20, 28, 40, 64, 65, 81, 82
Brand, Harry, 15
Breslow, Lou, 63-64, **64**, 69
Bridgeport *Telegram* (newspaper), 34
Bright Eyes (1934 film), 63, 65
Byron, Marion, 68-69

C

Callander Bay Heritage Museum, 83
Callander, Ontario, 9, 10, 11, 15, 21, 45, 49, 51, 55, 63, 65, 66, 68, 69, 70, 73
Canadian Broadcasting Company, 13

Captain Blood (1935 film), 28
Cantor, Eddie, 12
Captain Hates the Sea, The (film), 73
Captain January (1936 film), 43
Carlyle, Aileen, 29
Carnegie Hall, 11
Car 99 (film), 51
Carroll, Earl, 43-44
Cat Creeps, The (1930 film), 28
CBS Radio, 59
Century of Progress Exhibition, 9
Chandler, George, **23**, 29, 51
Chaplin, Charlie, 29, 61
Charlie Chan (movie series), 24
Charlie Chan at the Racetrack (film), 51
Chicago American (newspaper), 15
Christy, Earl, 39
Clare, Sidney, 65
Clark, Daniel B., 21, 23, 24, 26, 30, 47, 66, 69-73
College Rhythm (film), 44
College Scandal (film), 51
Collins, Claude, 40
Coo-Coo Nut Grove, The (cartoon short), 41
Cooper, Jackie, 44
Corriveau, Louise, 61, 73
Country Doctor, The (film)
    current availability, 83
    Dionne Quintuplets's fee for, 20-21, 27
    Dionne Quintuplets's footage in, 30, 32, 34, 36, 40, 46, 75
    filming Dionne Quintuplets's scenes, 20, 24-26, 46
    on television, 83

post-production, 30, 71

pre-production, 20, 67

production, *14, 16, 17, 18, 19, 21*, 22-30, 44-46, 51, 74

promotion, 22, 26, *29,* 31-32, *33, 35*

publicity stills, *23, 24, 25, 27, 28, 31*

release, 28, 30-34, 36, 37, 38, 43, 54, 56, 74, 81, 83

reviews, 32, 34, 36, 37, 55

writing, 15-19, 21

Courtney, Inez, 73, *74, 75*

Crisler, B.R., 61

Croll, David A., 20

Curly Top (1935 film), 29

D

Dafoe, Dr. Allan Roy

  as physician for the Dionne Quintuplets, 15; 16, 59, 72

  background, 10;

  celebrity, 10, 12, 31, 32, 38, 77, 82

  character of, 10, 17, 23, 24

  death, 82

  delivering the Dionne Quintuplets, 9

  endorsement deals, 11, 12, 18

  fees of, 11, 12, 18

  former home, 83

  lecturer, 11

  physical appearance of, 21

  radio appearances, 12, 13

  relationship with Dionne Quintuplets's parents, 27, 36, 65, 82

  work on *The Country Doctor, 14; 16, 18,* 20, 23, 24, 26, 36

  work on *Five of a Kind, 64,* 66, 70, 77

  work on *Reunion,* 45, 46, 47, 49

Dafoe Hospital, 10, 20, 46, 52, 54, 59, 64, 65, 67, 69, 71, 81, 82

Dante's Inferno (1935 film), 51, 63, 73

Darwell, Jane, 29, 74

Davis, Bette, 7, 12

Davis, Fred, 11, 23, 32, 46

Davis, Joan, 73

A Day at Home (short), *58,* 59-61

Day in the Lives of the Dionne Quintuplets, A, (short), 11

Day with the Dionne Quints, A, (short), 57

Dead End (film), 73

Dell Publishing, 61

Del Rio, Dolores, 63

Destry Rides Again (1932 film), 51

Devil Is a Woman (film), 73

Dietrich, Marlene, 73

Dimples (1936 film), 51

Dinehart, Alan, 51

Dinner at Eight (film), 21

Dionne, Annette (Quintuplet), 10, 45, 46, 59, 64, 77, 83

Dionne, Cecile (Quintuplet), 10, *22,* 26, 45, 46, 49, 59, 64, 77, 83

Dionne, Elzire (mother of Quintuplets)

  birth of Quintuplets, 9

  Chicago vaudeville tour, 11, 12

  control of Quintuplets, 81-82

  movie offers for, 27, 29, 30

  opinion of Quintuplets's movies, 27, 36, 65, 68, 70

  relationship with Dafoe, 27, 36, 65, 82

Dionne, Emilie (Quintuplet), 10, *43,* 45, 46, 49, 54, 59, 64, 77

  death of, 82

Dionne, Marie (Quintuplet), 10, 25, 46, 59, 64, 65, 67, 77

  death of, 82

Dionne, Oliva (father of Quintuplets)

  birth of Quintuplets, 9

  celebrity, 54, 59, 63, 65, 68

  Chicago vaudeville tour, 11, 12

  control of Quintuplets 81-82

  movie offers for, 27, 29, 30

  opinion of Quintuplets's movies, 27, 36, 52, 65, 67-68, 82

  relationship with Dafoe, 27, 36, 65, 82

  souvenir stand, *63,* 65, 68, 73

Dionne Quintuplets Dolls, 22, 32, 54
Dionne Quintuplets, The
  autobiography (1963) of, 11, 83
  birth, 9
  decline in popularity, 81-82
  development of, 46, 59, 65, 67, 72
  early care of, 8, 15
  endorsement deals, 11, 12, 57, 81, 82
  fees of, 7, 11, 12, 20, 2, 27, 40, 41, 51,
    56, 57, 63, 74, 81, 82
  fifth birthday, 81
  first birthday, 13
  fourth birthday, 81
  in *The Country Doctor*, *19*, 24-25, *28*,
    29, 30-32, *35*, 36, 38, 40, 44, 54
  in *Five of a Kind*, 64, *65*, 66-67, *68*,
    69, 70, *71*, 72-79, *78*
  in *Reunion*, *42*, 43, *44*, 45-49, *50*,
    51-52, *53*, 54, *55*, 56
  isolation of, 59, 70
  later years, 82-83
  legacy of film work, 7, 83
  movie contracts for, 11, 20, 40, 57
  movie costumes, *42*, 45, *53*, 54, 65-
    66, 70, 77
  movie offers for, 19-20, 38, 40
  newsreels of, 11, 13, 20, *22*, 23, 24,
    27, 30, 34, 40; *12*, *57*, *58*, 59-61, 62,
    64, 73, 79, 81, 82
  personalities of, 59, 62, 67, 70, 76
  proposed, unmade films, 56-57,
    81-82
  psychology of, 59
  public exhibition of, 10, 57, 59, 70, 82
  radio appearances, *10*, 13, 82
  second birthday, 40
  shooting still photos of, 11, 23, 24,
    32, 46, 57, 61-62
  speech of, 49, 59, 64, 71-72, 75-79,
    81, 82
  third birthday, 57
  singing and dancing of, 64-65, 76-79,
    82
  stage appearances, 82

Dionne Quintuplets, The
  (documentary), 24-25
Dionne Quintuplets at Play, The
  (short), 13
Dionne Quintuplets Dolls, *22*, 32, 54,
  57, 77, *78*, 81
Dionne Quintuplets Play Mother Goose
  (book), *60-61*
Dionne Years, The, (book) 9, 20
Dionne, Yvonne (Quintuplet), 10, 25,
  27, 46, 59, 64, 65, 77
  death of, 83
Don Juan (1926 film), 28
Donlevy, Brian, 63
Dr. Christian (movie series), 59
Dr. Christian (radio show), 59

E

Ernest, George, 51
Everybody's Old Man (film), 43
Everybody's Sweethearts (proposed film
  title), 63
Exhibitor, The (trade publication), 74

F

Farmer Takes a Wife, The (film), 29
Faye, Alice, 40, 45
Ferris, Walter, 43
Fields, W.C., 44
"Frere Jacques" (song), 76, 79
15 Maiden Lane (film), 73
Five of a Kind (film)
  costumes, 65-66, 70, 77
  current availability, 83
  Dionne Quintuplets's fee for, 63, 74
  Dionne Quintuplets's footage in, *67*,
    68, *68*, 70, *71*, 72-79
  Dionne Quintuplets's singing and
    dancing in, 64-65
  filming Dionne Quintuplets's scenes,
    69-71
  on television, 83

original title of, 63
post-production, 74
pre-production, 64, 66-67
production, 63, *64*, 66-76
promotion, 64, 66, *76*, 77
publicity stills, *66*, *72*, *74*, *75*, *78*;
release, 74, 77, 79, 81, 83
reviews, 74, 77-79;
writing, 63-64, 71, 73
Five Times Five (short), 81
Footlight Parade (film), 29
Four Horsemen of the Apocalypse, The
(film), 20
Fox-Movietone, 11, 75, 82
Freling, Fritz, 41

G

Garbo, Greta, 23
Going on Two (short), 40
Gould, Bruce, 43
Grand Hotel (film), 21
Grauman's Chinese Theater, 77
Greed (film), 20

H

Haden, Sara, *48*
Happy Landing (1938 film), 73
Hartford Times (newspaper), 36
Hee, T., 41
Hellman, Sam, 43
Henie, Sonja, 40, 45, 73
Hersholt, Jean
    between Dionne Quintuplets's films,
        59
    early career, 20-21
    in *The Country Doctor*, *14*, *16*, *17*, *19*;
        20-21, 23, *24*, 25-27, 30, *31*, 32, 38
    in *Five of a Kind*, *64*, *65*, *67*, 67 68,
        68, *69*, 70, *71*, 72-73, *74*, *75*, 77
    in *Reunion*, *44*, 45, *47*, *48*, 49, 52, 54,
        56
High Tension (film), 63

Hollywood, California, 12, 13, 15, 16,
    27, 30, 45, 51, 77
Hollywood (magazine), 45
Hollywood Reporter, The (trade
    publication), 36, 74
Holy Terror, The (film), 63
House of Rothschild (film), 16, 64
Hudson, Rochelle, *44*, 45, *47*, 49, 54
"Humpty Dumpty" (nursery rhyme), 61
Hurricane, The (film), 73

I

I Am a Fugitive From a Chain Gang
    (film), 51
Imitation of Life (1934 film), 45
I'm No Angel (film), 21
International Photographer (magazine),
    11
International Settlement (film), 63
Invisible Ray, The (film) 28
Island in the Sky (1938 film), 64

J

Johnson, Nunnally, 16, 18, 19, 21, 38, 43
Jones Family (movie series), 63, 64
Judge Priest (film), 51

K

Keaton, Buster, 68
Keep Smiling (1938 film), 64
Kennel Murder Case, The (film), 29, 51
Kent, Robert, *47*, 51-52
Kent, Sidney, 36
"Keystone Kops," 28
King, Henry, 17-18, 20-21, *21*, 23,
    25-26, 28, 30, 32, 38

L

Labelle, Benoit, 9
Lamoureux, Cecile, 23

Lang, June, *23*, 28, 45
Larson, LeVaughn, 70
Last of the Mohicans, The, (1936 film),
  28
Lee, Sonia, 49
Leeds, Herbert I., 64, *64*, 66, 70
Legion of Decency, 54
Legros, Alexandre, 9
Lehman, Gladys, 43
Leroux, Yvonne, *17*, *21*, 23, 52
Les Miserables (1935 film), 45
Levien, Sonja, 16-19, 21, 25, 36, 43
Life Begins in College (film), 73
Literary Digest (magazine), 38
Little Men (1934 film), 51
Little Miss Marker (1934 film), 43
Littlest Rebel, The (1935 film), 37
Lloyd, Harold, 19, 20
Lloyd's of London (film), 38, 43
Look (magazine), 77
Los Angeles Herald (newspaper), 34, 36
Love, Montagu, 28, 51, 74
Love on a Budget (film), 64

M

Madame Alexander Company, 32, 81
"Ma, He's Making Eyes at Me" (song),
  65
Marx, Groucho, 13
Mask of Fu Manchu, The (film), 21
Mata Hari (1932 film), 28
McDaniel, Hattie, 51
McLean, Barbara, 30
Miami Herald (newspaper), 34
Michaud, Cecile, 62
Milky Way, The (1936 film), 20
Milwaukee Sentinel (newspaper), 36
Mintz, Jack, 51
Modern Movies (magazine), 77
Modern Screen (magazine), *39*, 41
Moore, R.C., 67
Morning Eagle (newspaper), 34

Moskowitz, Joseph, 20-22, *64*, 67
Mother Knows Best (proposed, unmade
  film), 57
Motion Picture Herald (trade
  publication), 20, 31, 34, 36, 52, 74
Moulin Rouge (1934 film), 16
Movie Classic (magazine), 24, 38, 49,
  51, 54
Movie Mirror (magazine), 12, 19, 26, 38
Mr. Moto (movie series), 63
Mrs. Wiggs of the Cabbage Patch (film),
  44
Munro, Keith, 20
Murray, Jack, 52
Myron, Helen A., 65

N

National Telefilm Associates, 83
New Haven Register (newspaper), 36
Newspaper Enterprises of America
  (NEA), 11, 32, 57, 77, 81
New York Daily Mirror (newspaper), 34
New York Daily News (newspaper), 34
New York Journal (newspaper), 15
New York Times, The (newspaper), 34,
  55, 61, 78
Noel, Jacqueline, 52
North Bay Nugget (newspaper), 56
Nugent, Frank S., 34, 78

O

Oakie, Jack, 44
"Old King Cole" (nursery rhyme), 61
Oliver Twist (1922 film), 51
Ontario Night (radio show), 82
"On the Good Ship Lollipop" (song), 65
Oscar (Academy Award), 16, 30, 38,
  44, 73, 81
O'Shaughnessey, Mollie, 52, 73
Our Daily Bread (film), 29
Owen, Ruth Bryan, 38

P

Paramount Pictures, 16, 19, 20, 51
Pathe, 11, 13, 20, 28, 30, 40-41, 59-61, 75, 79, 81-82
Pathegrams, Inc., 60
Patrick, John, 63-64
Peck's Bad Boy (1934 film), 21
Peter Pan (1924 film), 51
Peterson, Dorothy, *16*, 21, 23, **24**, 25-26, **27**, **28**, 30, **31**, **43**, 45, **47**, 49, 51, 68
Photoplay (magazine), 12, 15, 54
Picture Play (magazine), 23, 67
Pittsburgh Sun-Telegraph (newspaper), 36
Pickford, Mary, 19, 20
Pigskin Parade (film), 43-44
Pluto's Quin-Puplets (cartoon short), 57
Pokrass, Samuel, 65
Poor Little Rich Girl (film), 43
Portland Express (newspaper), 34
Power, Tyrone, 52
Prisoner of Shark Island (film), 16, 52
Punch Drunks (short), 64

Q

Qualen, John, **25**, 29, 30, 34, 36, 51, 52, **72**, 73
Quintland, 11, 12,
Quint to Queens (book), 61
Quintupland (short), 61
Quintuplets' Second Christmas, The, (short), **22**, 28, 32

R

Radio City Music Hall, 32, 36
Raft, George, 64
Ralston, Esther, 51
Rebecca of Sunnybrook Farm (1932 film), 16
Reicher, Frank, 28

Reunion (film)
  costumes, **42**, 45, **53**, 54
  current availability, 83
  Dionne Quintuplets's fee for, 51, 56
  Dionne Quintuplets's footage in, 44, 49, 51-52, 55-56, 75
  filming Dionne Quintuplets's scenes, 45-49
  on television, 83
  original title of, 43
  post-production, 52, 71
  pre-production, 44
  production, **42**, **43**, **44**, 45-49, 51-52, 73
  promotion, 44, **50**, **51**, **53**, 54, **55**
  publicity stills, **47**, **48**
  release, 52, 54, 56, 81, 83
  reviews, 52, 55-56
  writing, 43, 45-46, 48, 51, 67, 73
Rin-Tin-Tin, 38
RKO Radio Pictures, 20, 59
"Rock-a-Bye, Baby" (nursery rhyme), 61
Rogers, Bogart, 43-44
Rogers, Will, 15, 17, 19-20, 45, 63
Roman Catholic Church, 36
Romero, Cesar, **72**, 73
Rouselle, Nora, 64
Royer, Luis, 45
Russell, Johnny, 75

S

Samrich, Mila, 44
Scarlet Empress, The (film), 29
Screen Romances (magazine), 54, 77
Sedgwick, Joseph, 20
Seitz, John F., 30
Show Boat (1936 film), 51
"Silly Symphonies" (cartoon short series)
Silver Screen (magazine), 77
Skippy (film), 44
State Fair (1933 film), 16, 17

Steamboat Bill, Jr. (film), 68
Steamboat 'Round the Bend (film), 63
Stella Dallas (1925 film), 17, 21
Stella Dallas (1937 film), 77
Stewart, James, 12, 52
St. Louis Post-Dispatch (newspaper), 36
Stolen Harmony (film), 64
Stowaway (1936 film), 44
Stuart, Gloria, 64
Summerville, Slim, *24*, 28, 30, 51, 52,
   56, *72*, 73
Sunshine Susie (film), 23

T

Tash, Roy, 11, 40
Taurog, Norman, *42*, *43*, 44-49, 51, 54
Temple, Shirley, 12, 37-38, 40, 43-45,
   51, 54, 56, 63-65, 70, 73, 76
They Always Come Back (proposed
   film title), 43
Thin Ice (film), 73
Thin Man, The (film), 73
This Side of Heaven (film), 29
Three Stooges, The, 13, 64
Time (magazine), 32, 78
Tol'able David (1921 film), 17
Toledo News-Bee (newspaper), 34
Torrence, David, 74
Treasure Island (1934 film), 21
Trevor, Claire, 73, *74*, *75*, 76
Twentieth-Century Fox (a.k.a. Fox), 7,
   15, 20, 30-32, 36-38, 40, 44-45,
   51-52, 54, 57, 63-64, 66, 69-70,
   73-76, 81-83; "B-picture" unit,
   63-64, 73-74

U

UCLA Film and Television Archive, 83
Ulrichson, Sigrid, 73
Under Two Flags (1936 film), 43
Universal Pictures, 27

V

Valle, Rudy, 12
Valin, J.A., 19
Variety (trade publication), 32, 34, 56,
   77
Vinson, Helen, 51

W

Walt Disney Studios, 57
Warner Brothers, 41
Wee Willie Winkie (film), 73
We Were Five (book), 11
Webb, Robert, 21
Werker, Alfred L., 64
Whalen, Michael, *23*, 28, 51
Where Are My Children? (proposed,
   unmade film), 27
Whiting, Richard, 65
Wilson, Harold, 43-44
Withers, Jane, 40, 63, 64, 65
Woman's Home Companion
   (magazine) 23
World War II, 81
Wurtzel, Sol M., 63-64, 66, 73
"Wyatt Quintuplets, The," 27, 43, 64,
   73, 75

Z

Zanuck, Darryl F., 7, 15-19, 21, 27-28,
   30, 38, 40, 43-45, 51, 56-57, 63-65,
   81-82

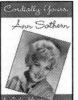

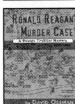

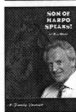

Printed in the United States
107456LV00001B/4-30/A